Loving
CHRIST

Also by Joseph M. Stowell

Following Christ

JOSEPH M. STOWELL

Loving
CHRIST

ECAPTURING YOUR PASSION FOR JESUS

ZondervanPublishingHouse
Grand Rapids, Michigan

A Division of HarperCollinsPublishers

We want to hear from you. Please send your comments about this book
to us in care of the address below. Thank you.

ZondervanPublishingHouse
Grand Rapids, Michigan 49530
http://www.zondervan.com

Loving Christ
Copyright © 2000 by Joseph M. Stowell

Requests for information should be addressed to:

 ZondervanPublishingHouse
Grand Rapids, Michigan 49530

ISBN: 0–310–21564–1

This edition printed on acid-free paper.

Interior design by Sue Vandenberg Koppenol

Printed in the United States of America

00 01 02 03 04 05 06 /❖ DC/ 10 9 8 7 6 5 4 3 2 1

To the students at Moody Bible Institute,
whose fresh and energetic love for Jesus
inspires and refreshes my desire
to love Him more

CONTENTS

WITH THANKS . . .

If your life is impacted by this book, then please thank . . .

Jesus, without whose matchless love we would never be able to enjoy the privilege of a loving relationship with Him.

Martie, my wife, whose interest in seeing this material getting into your hands meant that she often had to endure the hardships of being a "book widow" as I got lost in the process of finishing this project.

My friends at Zondervan Publishing House, who understand the dilemma of my overcrowded life and graciously extended deadlines to accommodate it.

Jack Kuhatschek, for mentoring me in my writing and helping to organize the thoughts and concepts in ways that more effectively communicate.

Jim Ruark, for his superb hand in the process of the final editing.

Lori Imhof, whose service to my ministry as executive secretary helped keep the decks clear so that this book could be written.

And, last but certainly not least, Charlotte Arman, who faithfully helped with research and gave oversight to the finished drafts and details of each chapter.

PREFACE

I am struck by the fact that Jesus, in His last conversation with Peter, was most interested in whether or not Peter loved Him. If Christ were to talk with you today, there is no doubt that He would be interested in the same issue. Our quick reply would certainly be like Peter's: "Of course, you know I love you!" But Christ would want things to go deeper than just our words. Our love for Him is best proven in the lives we live. And, we must add, loving Him is not a throwaway issue to be done or not to be done at our own pleasure.

From the very first description of God's intentions regarding our relationship with Him, it becomes apparent that it is not just to be another religious arrangement predominantly characterized by rituals and legally binding arrangements. Although aspects of those stabilizing functions will be involved, it is to be first and foremost a relationship built on mutual love. First there is *His* surprising and undeserved love for us, the offensively fallen ones, and then *our* love, which is to spring forth as a grateful response.

A quick survey would reveal that many of us have not yet gotten a grip on this priority dynamic of our faith. Love for Christ as a reality that drives and defines all that we do . . . that makes us glad to not do what we should not do . . . seems to be in short supply. Our Christianity is usually lived out on lesser planes of "have to" and habit. Hence the lack of vitality and the regular sense that our relationship with Jesus is often flat and sometimes tedious.

Loving Christ is about learning to enjoy the liberating dynamic of a life moved by love. Our unlikely teacher is the sinning woman in Luke 7. Our look-a-like unfortunately is Simon Good Guy, who, though well conformed to proper behavior, gets low grades on loving. His attitudes at times create uncomfortable comparisons to our own loveless ways of living.

This book is a sequel to *Following Christ.* Once we have truly decided to follow Him, learning to love Him provides the will and energy to happily stay in the process. It is my prayer that after reading this book your life will be indelibly marked by a growing love that will not let you go.

Loving CHRIST

Now one of the Pharisees invited Jesus to have dinner with him, so he went to the Pharisee's house and reclined at the table. When a woman who had lived a sinful life in that town learned that Jesus was eating at the Pharisee's house, she brought an alabaster jar of perfume, and as she stood behind him at his feet weeping, she began to wet his feet with her tears. Then she wiped them with her hair, kissed them and poured perfume on them.

When the Pharisee who had invited him saw this, he said to himself, "If this man were a prophet, he would know who is touching him and what kind of woman she is—that she is a sinner."

Then he turned toward the woman and said to Simon, "Do you see this woman? I came into your house. You did not give me any water for my feet, but she wet my feet with her tears and wiped them with her hair. You did not give me a kiss, but this woman, from the time I entered, has not stopped kissing my feet. You did not put oil on my head, but she has poured perfume on my feet. Therefore, I tell you, her many sins have been forgiven—for she loved much. But he who has been forgiven little loves little."

Then Jesus said to her, "Your sins are forgiven."

—Luke 7:36–39, 44–48

CHAPTER ONE

AT JESUS' FEET

Life Among the Forgiven Much

Ruth McBride Jordan lives in a cozy home in a lovely part of New Jersey, near Trenton. At the ripe age of seventy-six, she graduated from Temple University with a degree in social work administration. She travels widely, serves in the homeless shelter of Jerusalem Baptist Church, and runs a reading program at the local library.

With a sense of appropriate pride, her son James tells her story in his best-selling book, *The Color of Water.* He relates that not only is she the mother of twelve grown children and the grandmother of twenty, but all of her children have earned college and graduate degrees and have distinguished themselves in their professions. That is an unusual track record for any parent, but it is all the more unusual because Ruth had reared her children during the tough years of the sixties in New York City, a time when racial unrest and lack of clear identity led many children to the streets and to far less stellar outcomes. Beyond that, the most amazing fact is that Ruth raised her children alone as a white Jewish woman in Harlem. Her husband, a black Baptist pastor, died early, leaving her with nothing but the resolve and motivation to do the best that she could in the midst of impossible circumstances.

Against the backdrop of her childhood, her story becomes even more amazing.

Ruth's father, a Polish immigrant, was an itinerant orthodox Jewish rabbi in Virginia. Her mother was a shy invalid who spoke little English and was often physically abused by her husband. Leaving the itinerant ministry, Tateh, as Ruth called her father, opened a general store in which Ruth was forced to work long hours. He treated her as a contribution to his economic success, and he also abused her sexually. Although she loved her mother deeply, she found little solace in her mom's frail and intimidated spirit.

As a result, Ruth spent most of her adolescent years looking for love outside her family. The search led her down dark and dangerous paths. She fell in love with a neighboring African-American boy who often shopped in the store. For the first time in her life she felt as though someone cared for her. However, this discovery of love proved unsafe. She became pregnant and risked the wrath of the small town in which her dad's store was located. Her mom sent her to New York City to spend some time with her aunt so the problem could be "dealt with."

Returning home, Ruth found that life would never again be the same. As soon as she finished high school, she ran back to New York and got a job in her aunt's leather factory. There she met Rocky and once again felt loved. She reveled in the warmth and affection of someone who cared for her—only to discover that he was a pimp, wooing her to become part of his harem.

As she fled this, another disastrous encounter with love, Ruth met Dennis McBride. There was something unusually authentic about his affections. This time she was wonderfully loved and was confident of it. Ruth felt safe and valued as he transferred a sense of dignity and worth to her lost and lonely soul.

But the secret to her dramatic recovery from a disastrous history did not come from her husband's love, as wonderful as it was. He died, leaving her a penniless widow in a Harlem flat, overcrowded with kids.

Her strength and resolve came from another man, a man Dennis had introduced her to.

Years later, Ruth told her son James the secret—the secret that enabled her to rise like a phoenix out of the ashes of her dad's abuse. "I was afraid of Tateh and had no love for him at all," she told James. "It affected me in a lot of ways, what he did to me. I had very low self-esteem as a child, which I kept with me for many, many years; and even now I don't want to be around anyone who is domineering or pushing me around, because it makes me nervous."

Ruth reflected on the harsh and insensitive slurs of those who decried her marrying a black man. "Well, I don't care. Your father changed my life. He taught me about God, who lifted me up and forgave me and made me new. I was lucky to meet him or I would've been a prostitute or dead. Who knows what would've happened to me? I was reborn in Christ. Had to be, after all I went through."[1]

James writes that during one of her most difficult times, "Ma was utterly confused about all but one thing: Jesus. . . . Jesus gave Mommy hope. Jesus was Mommy's salvation. Jesus pressed her forward. Each and every Sunday, no matter how tired, depressed or broke, she got up early, dressed in her best, and headed for church."[2]

He recalls, "Even as a boy I knew God was all powerful because of Mommy's utter deference to him, and also because she would occasionally do something in church that I never saw her do at home or anywhere else: at some point in the service, usually when the congregation was singing one of her favorite songs like, 'We've Come This Far by Faith' or 'What a Friend We Have in Jesus,' she would bow down her head and weep. It was the only time I saw her cry. 'Why do you cry in church?' I asked her one afternoon after the service. 'Because God makes me happy. . . . I'm crying 'cause I'm happy.'"[3]

How do the Ruths of this world manage to come through with hands held high in victory? What is the secret to rising above the debilitating effects of brokenness, burdens, bondage, temptation, and all the other things that life so often inflicts upon us? At the other end of the spectrum, is there any hope to escape the numbing effect that good times can have on our spiritual sensitivities? Is it possible to dodge the distractions of prosperity and still function as authentic cutting-edge followers of Christ?

The answer is clear . . . and the answer holds our only hope. It is a love for Christ so compelling that it drives and defines all that we do—a love that is defined by the life-changing goodness that Christ brings to our existence. When our love for Christ moves beyond a mere mental assent to a living reality, it motivates us to deal with life in unique and powerful ways, regardless of our circumstances.

When our love for Christ moves beyond a mere mental assent to a living reality, it motivates us to deal with life in unique and powerful ways, regardless of our circumstances.

We shouldn't be surprised. People do crazy things for love. They leave families or change careers. Country music fans start going to the opera. Macho men discover flower shops and perfume counters. Lovers say weird things and make unbelievable promises. They leave old friends and get involved with new. Some reject wealth and choose to live in shacks in the wilderness. People kill for love. Some have died for it.

BOLD ADORATION

Ruth McBride's grateful love for Christ is a modern-day version of another Jewish woman who lived nearly two thousand years ago. She, too, expressed her love to Christ in bold acts of adoration. In fact, her love was so compelling that first-century followers were inspired to go and live likewise each time her story was read in their gatherings. Their mutual commitment to let their lives be driven by a similar love for Christ eventually brought the Roman Empire to its knees.

We are introduced to this woman by the gospel writer Luke, who in thirteen verses describes what might be Scripture's most moving and instructive picture of what it means to love Christ. We are never told her name, but Luke says she was a woman "who had lived a sinful life" (Luke 7:37). Luke doesn't say exactly what gave her such a bad reputation, but the word he uses to describe her—"sinner"—is most often used in reference to people whose lives were characterized by immorality. She was probably the town prostitute or, at best, a woman known for having loose morals. In that Jewish culture, being a "sinner" marked her as a social outcast and placed her among the lowest and most despised people in town.

Her mention in the passage is not the most striking feature. We often read of sinners being present where Jesus is ministering. The most notable feature is that she shows up in the home of Simon the Pharisee. He is clearly the best, most religious, most publicly revered person in town. What she does that evening in his home offends every fiber of his Pharisaism, his commitment to purity and propriety. At this point, Luke has done what he is fond of doing: taking the worst of sinners and putting them into the mix with people who were the most moral. The resulting juxtaposition shows the strength and breadth of God's love for the worst of us while at the same time reflecting the ever-present prejudices of our small and self-centered hearts.

This sinner-saint encounter is intended to place in bold relief the huge distance between the sinful woman and self-righteous Simon. In fact, one of the primary purposes of this text is to reveal how far we, the "good people," may be from loving God. It is a scary thought to realize that well-intentioned good people might be clueless about loving Christ and can even become offensive to Him in their goodness. But that is exactly what Simon teaches us.

Luke's account probes the essence of what it means to love Christ. It forces us to consider whether we are more like the loving woman or the standoffish, self-congratulating Simon. Of course, we immediately want to believe that we would be at the feet of Jesus competing for space with the woman. Chances are, most of us are more like Simon. If that thought troubles you, then we are off to a good start. Wanting to love

Him in authentic ways that connect with His heart is the beginning of a satisfying relationship with Christ that provides the power to live a transformed life.

AMAZING LOVE

As the drama unfolds, we can't help but be amazed at the stunning quality of the woman's love. It's courageous, bold, and quick to express itself regardless of the environment or the expectations of others.

Hearing that Jesus is dining with Simon the Pharisee, the woman grabs her most prized possession and makes her way to Simon's house. Our first response might be that she is quite rude, since she has not been invited to the dinner. However, it is not unusual for the citizens of a town to crowd around the walls or portico of the room where dinners like this are being held. Occasions of this sort are major events. They would be held in large dining rooms or in the courtyards of the homes of famous people. The guest list would include only the rich and important. Just as nowadays people stand along sidewalks to get a glimpse of famous people, so it would be customary for the doors of Simon's home to be open to anyone who wants to watch and listen to all that is going on.

These dinners typically last well into the night. The invited guests would lounge on couches as they eat and spend the evening in deep conversations about social issues, local politics, philosophy, or national affairs. Tonight the topic of discussion would obviously be theology, since Jesus is there, and perhaps there would even be a polite yet pointed probing of His claim to be the Messiah. For the common citizens of the town, an event like this is an exciting affair in their pre-television, pre–let's-go-to-the-movies world.

So for this woman to be there is not unusual.

What is unusual is what happens next. She steps from the crowd and moves toward the reclining guests. You can be sure that at this point the clattering noises of the busy servants stop, side conversations at the table suddenly become irrelevant, and the buzzing among the gathered townspeople trails off as all eyes become fixed on her. No doubt guests and observers alike elbow each other and point to her as she moves from the crowd to the dining room. Everyone knows who she is. In fact, some people no doubt know her quite well. For *her* to invade the space of the invited guests sends a curious chill over the evening. Furthermore, Simon, who has been busy engaging the guests and managing the servants, is no doubt stunned into a state of shock. This evening is not going as he had planned.

What she does next not only steals the show but also flies in the face of tradition and the finely tuned religious sensitivities of Simon and his guests. In spite of the stares from the crowd and Simon's disapproving glare, she picks her way through the guests, looking for Jesus. Finding Him, she stops at His feet—where the servant of the house would normally stand—and breaks the suspense with deep sobs that find her tears falling on Jesus' feet. She loosens her hair to wipe the tears as she bows at His feet and kisses them over and over again. Then the heavy, alluring fragrance of perfume penetrates the room—which has been full of the aroma of the wine, figs, and lavishly prepared food—as she opens her alabaster vial and anoints His feet. This is a fragrance that may have embarrassingly reminded some of the guests of earlier trysts with her.

Count on it, Simon is scandalized! Before the meal, he would have performed ritualistic cleansings to purify himself according to the traditions of the pharisaical code. For a woman—any woman, but particularly a woman of this character—to step out and lovingly anoint Jesus in the presence of Simon and his guests is abhorrent to his sense of propriety and purity. It simply is not religiously correct. He has no space in his system of righteousness for bold and beautiful expressions of love that come from a heart unfamiliar with the codified constructs of "goodness."

Simon has no space in his system of righteousness for bold and beautiful expressions of love that come from a heart unfamiliar with the codified constructs of "goodness."

What is so admirable about this woman's act of adoring love is that it is played out with unusual courage and a refreshingly innocent audacity. A woman of her tainted reputation can expect nothing but judgment and rejection in Simon's presence. She is little more than a marginalized outcast. Yet, lost in her love for Jesus, she rushes into the presence of her self-righteous accusers and acts out her grateful affection for Him. Her love for Jesus is an overwhelming compulsion. It prompts her to transcend the ordinary with acts of affection and adoration that catch the attention of even the most cynical onlooker.

If you were Jewish and living in Jesus' day, you would know how surprisingly bold and radical this act of love really is, which is what seemingly puts Jesus in a bind. He is now caught in the convergence of an authentic love that is on a collision course with deeply rooted religious norms and cultural expectations.

THE FRIEND OF SINNERS

Jesus, as the object of her adoring attention, is now forced into an unfortunate turn of events. The crowd—its attention riveted on this sensual woman—suddenly turns its focus on Jesus to see how He will respond. Since Simon holds all the power in town, it would be expedient for Jesus to side with the Pharisee by resisting the woman's overtures of love. She has clearly crossed the limits of what is appropriate, and no one would be surprised if Jesus chooses to resist her. In fact, if He accepts her acts of love, Jesus risks marginalizing Himself, eroding His credibility with the mesmerized crowd, and offending the influential Simon. Accepting her love would play into the already prevalent thought among the religious leaders that Jesus is not one of their kind.

We all know how difficult it is to resist playing to those who have power and privilege. Who of us would not have wanted to be accepted by the prestigious group that had been invited to the table that night? Jesus has everything to gain by pushing the woman aside and everything to lose by affirming her devotion. In fact, if Jesus plays the moment correctly, He can turn it to His advantage. By casting His lot with the power broker Simon He might be able to glean an endorsement for His ministry in town, or at least minimize the accusation that He is no more than an itinerant revolutionary peasant who is outside the loop of legitimacy.

Yet Jesus resists what would have been the choice of lesser men. Without hesitation He affirms her love and becomes the sole defender of this despised woman. One thing is clear: Her response to Jesus, though radical and culturally abhorrent, has touched His heart. He feels loved by her and becomes, as He always is, the advocate of loving souls who express their love to Him in authentic ways, regardless of how desperately sinful they may be. As the story unfolds, it becomes abundantly clear that Jesus is indeed a friend of sinners.

THE FORGIVEN MUCH

What is it that has given rise to such a radical and risky expression of love for Jesus from such an unlikely person? If we can answer that question, we stand a chance of discovering what we need in our hearts to stimulate a similar life-transforming love.

Jesus is quick to explain her love to the shocked Simon by telling him a story of two debtors. One owed a great deal to a moneylender, and the other owed considerably less. But since neither of them could repay, the lender graciously forgave them both. Jesus then asks Simon if he knows which debtor would love the moneylender more: the one who was forgiven much, or the one who was forgiven little? Simon responds, "The one who is forgiven more." Jesus congratulates Simon for answering correctly and then turns the point of the story toward Simon himself.

In a withering reproof, Jesus confronts Simon with his obvious lack of love. Simon has not extended to Jesus even the most common of courtesies. Jesus is an invited guest, yet Simon has not summoned a servant to wash His feet. Nor has he greeted Jesus with a kiss on the cheek or forehead, which is the custom in welcoming guests to one's home. These acts of courtesy are like asking if I may hang up your coat if you were to visit our home in the winter; if I don't ask for your coat, my silence suggests that you aren't really welcome. As we will see, there may be reasons why Simon has withheld these routine gestures of hospitality, but in this cultural setting he has acted in a rude and offensive way toward Jesus. We can be quite sure that Jesus is the only invited guest to have been denied these gestures.

Jesus obviously has not missed the snub. He not only notes that His feet have gone unwashed and His cheek unkissed, but also reminds Simon that he has not anointed His head with oil. This is a grace bestowed on special guests to honor their presence. In the homes of the poor, it is a simple anointing with less expensive oils. But in a home like Simon's, expensive oils are used, filled with the fragrance of exotic herbs and spices. The clothes of the anointed guest would be drenched with the anointing as the oil flows onto the shoulders, and for the rest of the evening and for days to come, the aroma of the honor remains with the celebrated guest.

It goes without saying that Simon does not feel it is appropriate to honor Jesus with an anointing on this occasion. But as Jesus graphically points out, this despised woman of the streets has washed His feet with her tears and has not stopped kissing His feet since the time she entered Simon's home. And, Jesus adds poignantly, she has also anointed His feet with her precious perfume.

All of this brings us to recognize where this outpouring of love comes from. Jesus says, "Therefore, I tell you, her many sins have been forgiven—for she loved much." Then, for Simon's benefit, He concludes, "But he who has been forgiven little loves little" (Luke 7:47).

Although the English text seems to indicate that her forgiveness is a result of her loving acts toward Christ, most scholars agree that the best rendering leaves us with the sense that the woman loves not to be forgiven but because she has already been forgiven. Not only is this consistent with the grammatical context, but it also most consistently parallels the meaning of the story that Christ has just told. The debtor loves because he has been forgiven much. Nowhere in Scripture do we find that loving Christ is the reason for forgiveness. Love for Him is always a response to having been forgiven. In essence Jesus tells Simon that those who have been forgiven much, love much.

This sinful woman loves this way because she belongs to a particular class of people. Those who find themselves in this class instinctively live life from the energy of a love for Jesus. She belongs to those who are among the *forgiven much*.

> *This sinful woman loves this way because she belongs to a particular class of people. She is among the forgiven much.*

MARVELOUS GRACE

One wonders what sermon Jesus was preaching at this point in His ministry that so deeply impacted this woman's heart and gave her hope that she too might find grace for her troubled soul. Unfortunately, Luke does not tell us what she has heard from Jesus, though he does give us a hint. Earlier in this chapter, Luke records that at about this time, John the Baptist sent his disciples to check out the credentials of Jesus. Matthew's gospel reveals what sermon Jesus was preaching.

Stand with this sinful woman in the crowd on that day when her town is buzzing with excitement about the arrival of this preacher who has taken the countryside by storm. She no doubt has heard, perhaps even from a customer who was traveling through town, about this Jesus who heals the sick and restores sight to the blind. She may even have heard, as strange as it would seem to her, that He has proven to be a friend of searching sinners. Coming to join the crowd—for she would have a Zacchaeus-type curiosity (Luke 19:1–4)—she strains to see and hear this Jesus. She catches a glimpse of His face, which seems to her to be the face of a man unlike any she has seen before. And, if you are her, think of the chord that the words that Matthew reports would have struck in your heavy heart:

"Come to me, all you who are weary and burdened, and I
will give you rest. Take my yoke upon you and learn from
me, for I am gentle and humble in heart, and you will find
rest for your souls. For my yoke is easy and my burden is
light" (Matt. 11:28–30).

We have to stop and process what it would mean for *this* woman
to hear such a welcoming, forgiving, merciful invitation like this from
Jesus. It was *she* who offered rest to men, in encounters that only left
her more laden with guilt. No one offered her rest. No one cared for her
soul. Men used and discarded her as an object of desire, or ruthlessly
condemned her. Any sense of worth and self-esteem were nonexistent
for her. She labored under the burden of inextricable guilt, weighed
down by the sludge of sin that polluted her soul. No one needed to tell
her how lost she was. She lived with that painful awareness every day.
What she needed was someone to tell her that there was a way out, a
way to be forgiven.

*No one needed to tell her how lost she was. What
she needed was someone to tell her that there was a
way out, a way to be forgiven.*

And now, for what may have been the first time in her life, the
woman comes in contact with a man who offers her forgiveness and a
love she can trust. She sees something different in His face. It is not the
look of curious desire that she has seen on the faces of so many others.
In her heart she senses that she can feel safe with a man like this. Has
she finally found someone who cares—someone who wants, not to use
her, but to bless her?

Later, as the crowd disperses, she lingers to ask about the invitation that Jesus has offered in His sermon. Could it be that she qualifies?
Does He understand who she is? Does it matter . . . as it has for most of
her life? Surprisingly, He is willing to talk with her. His look and His

voice raise her hope that she might find grace in His sight. She hears what for her are almost unbelievable words. Unlike what she had been taught all her life, she hears that God is a God of mercy and grace who delights in forgiving those who come to Him seeking forgiveness and restoration.

She knows in a heartbeat that this is not only what she wants but also what she needs. For too long she has been the object of men's damaging lusts. Now she glimpses an opportunity to become the object of a man's redeeming love. And in a moment of unqualified belief, the sludge that has for so long clogged her soul with guilt and self-incrimination is driven away by the cleansing presence of His promise as the Spirit-breathed clean sweet air of forgiveness fills her transformed soul.

Is it any wonder that when she hears that Jesus is still in town and dining at the Pharisee's home, she says to herself, "I have to go and see Him once again . . . to tell Him how much I love Him!" Making her way through the streets that used to be the dark passages of her trade, she sets out to express a new kind of love that is unstained by the past. Arriving at Simon's house, she is shocked by the rude and insensitive treatment that Jesus has received, and without giving it another thought, she breaks from the margins of the room and serves Him with loving acts that the most religious man in town refused to extend.

Why? Because she is among the *forgiven much*. And as Christ has taught us, those who are forgiven much love much.

As Christ has taught us, those who are forgiven much love much.

For her, as it must be for all of us, adoring expressions of love for Him are stimulated by His life-liberating love for us. He had stunned her heart with His marvelous forgiving grace, and now she searches for ways to say thank you in courageous, reciprocal acts of love.

Had she known these hymns, they would have been the anthems of her release:

O to grace how great a debtor daily I'm constrained to be!
Let Thy goodness like a fetter bind my wandering heart to
Thee.

or,

Love so amazing, so divine, demands my soul, my life, my all.

or,

And can it be that I should gain an interest in the Savior's
blood?
Died He for me, who caused His pain? For me, who Him
to death pursued?
Amazing love! How can it be that Thou, my God, shouldst
die for me? . . .

My chains fell off, my heart was free, I rose, went forth, and
followed Thee.

RESPONSIVE LOVE

Mark it down: Loving Christ is a response—a response to His
enduring, unwarranted love for us. His amazing grace motivates us like
nothing else to live out our lives in unique and, when necessary, courageous ways that express our deep affection and honor for Him before
a watching and often critical world. Why would you or I forgive a parent who had abused us? Why would anyone endure a difficult marriage
out of conviction that it is the right and best thing to do? Why do
Sudanese Christians permit themselves to be sold into slavery rather
than deny the name of Christ? Why do people leave lucrative and highly
applauded positions to take some paltry task in the kingdom work of
Christ? Why have martyrs gladly died and others lived in terrible situ-
ations with a good and uncompromised spirit? Believe me, this self-
lessness does not arise out of a sense of obligation. Duty does not provide

sufficient resolve. When the chips are down or the stakes are high, mere commitment is rarely enough to lead us through to victory.

We are able to do these things when we are motivated to express a loyal and undying love for Christ. Since He has lovingly and enduringly done so much for them, lovers of Christ thrive on opportunities to express their love to Him in return.

So as Christ-lovers we must ask, "Where am I on the continuum between the Pharisee and the immoral woman?" Probe your recent past. When was the last time you were willing to do something radical and dramatic to express your overflowing love for Christ? Is there a momentum in your soul toward a deepening, life-altering love for Christ, or are you still stuck in a cognitive, codified passionless arrangement with Him? The answers to these questions determine the authenticity and integrity of our claim to be lovers of Christ.

To love Christ, to really love Him, means that like the sinful woman we seek ways to express our love to Christ aggressively and without intimidation—regardless. It is gratitude toward a forgiving and grace-extending Savior that drives us to seek out ways to say, "Thank you! This is how much I love you."

FREE AT LAST

What really bothered Ruth McBride Jordan was her deep guilt for not having gone to be with her mother before she died. While her family had officially rejected her and refused to tell her where her mother was, Ruth blamed herself for deserting her mom and deeply grieved the lack of closure. She says,

> I was depressed for months. I lost weight and couldn't eat and was near suicide. I kept saying, "Why couldn't it have been me that died?" . . . Dennis was the one who shook me out of it. He kept saying, "You've got to forgive yourself, Ruth. God forgives you. He'll forgive the most dreaded sin, the most dreaded sin." But I couldn't listen, not for a long

while, I couldn't listen. I was so, so sorry. Deep in my heart I was sorry. . . . Lord, I was burning with hurt. . . . I didn't think she was dying when I left home but she knew it. . . . All her life I was the one who translated for her and helped her around, I was her eyes and her ears in America, and when I left . . . well, . . . her husband treated her so bad and divorced her, and her reasons for living just slipped away. It was a bad time.

It took a long time to get over it, but Dennis stuck it out with me, and after a while I began to listen to what he said about God forgiving you and I began to hold on to that, that God will forgive you, will forgive the most dreaded sin.[4]

When Ruth realized that God had lifted the burden of her sin by bearing it Himself on the cross, she turned her eyes and heart toward Him as Savior, Redeemer, Liberator, and Friend. She never recovered from the impact of His love for her. And she never stopped gratefully expressing it to Him in sacrificial love to a brood of kids whose lives now bless thousands of people across America.

Ruth lived out her life in the face of great odds as a member of that select group of those who have been *forgiven much*. And her love for Christ saw her through.

CHAPTER TWO

LOVE THE WAY IT WAS MEANT TO BE

The Responsibility and the Response

I hope I never grow too old to remember the glorious days when I started to fall in love with Martie. I loved to catch sight of her across campus or see her on the way to class. I fretted about whether or not she liked me as much as I liked her. Walking with her made life seem more than wonderful. We talked about anything and everything. Regardless of the topic, it all seemed both enthralling and profound. The greatest risk was wondering if I should take her hand. The excitement of our hands accidentally touching seems almost silly now, but then it was filled with a mysterious significance. The first kiss . . . the moment I first said, "I love you."

By the end of our freshman year in college, I knew she was the one I wanted—no, *needed*—to marry. I couldn't wait to tell my father.

As we sat under the old apple tree in our backyard, I had two things to share with him. The first was that I had blown up a toilet in

29

the dorm after a discussion with my roommate over whether or not fire-crackers went off underwater. He needed to know this, since I had to come up with the money to cover the damage. The second issue pressing my heart was Martie and the fact I had found the one I wanted to marry. Or, more precisely and more convincingly to my father, that the Lord had led me to the most wonderful woman in the whole world—the one I wanted to be with for the rest of my life.

I am sure Dad couldn't quite put together the sharp contrast between someone who blows up toilets to settle an argument and someone who is at the same time mature enough to be so sure about his life partner. But to his credit, Dad took both pieces of news in stride.

What troubled me was not what my father said about the underwater experiment, but what he asked me about Martie. He asked how I knew I was in love. I remember giving him a list of her unsurpassed qualities and then feeling totally inadequate to describe and define how I really felt about her. Trying to describe and define love is like trying to explain how a great golf shot feels or what the sound of a shallow, quick babbling brook does for your soul.

Which is why the question of a graduate student left me feeling so inadequate.

WHAT DOES LOVE MEAN?

As we chatted over a cup of coffee, the student asked me the ultimate question, "What does it *really* mean to love God?" He could not have asked a more profoundly important question. I have to admit that I was somewhat surprised at the question, given that he was a graduate student in theology. But in fairness to him, my guess is that most of us faced with the same question would have a difficult time coming up with a clear and concise answer that could be readily transferred to life.

I felt inadequate because trying to define love, particularly love for the Divine, is bound to injure our understanding of it. Some things are too grand and too rich to try to reduce them to a definitive statement. Quarantining love into the confines of even the worthiest definition threatens to leave it flat and dull.

The brilliance and beauty of love are expressed and experienced in as many ways as there are people. Some of us enjoy and express it cognitively while others get in touch with it emotionally. Love is expressed by some in intangible ways, and by others in the tangible world of words, songs, and flowers. A wink across a crowded room can carry the power of a nuclear explosion in the heart of the recipient. For someone else, only a dozen red roses or a box of chocolates will do.

Yet the reality that love defies description does not mean we are left to love any old way we please. Love does have *boundaries*. Having an affair may be about making love or feeling loved, but it is not a loving act in the end, certainly not to our spouse, children, and others to whom we are responsible. Living for self and ignoring the needs and expectations of those around me may be about self-love, but it is not real love.

> *There is a richness to love that is to be* pursued *if we are to enjoy its benefits to the full.*

Moreover, love is about more than boundaries. If we are to master the art of loving, we must do more than simply stay within the boundaries. There is a richness to love that is to be *pursued* if we are to enjoy its benefits to the full. Marriage, for example, is best experienced not as a duty with limits, but as a pursuit of a relationship that is filled with the kind of affection and adoration that propel us toward pleasing our partner in loving acts of service and sometimes sacrifice.

Scripture teaches that cultivating a love relationship with Christ follows the same pattern. God's Word sets clear boundaries for our love to Him and a target within the boundary for us to pursue. It's like archery. The aim is not just to stay within the concentric circles (though that is better than missing the target altogether), but to zero in on the bull's-eye.

BLESSING THE BOUNDARIES

If you and I were to tackle the seminarian's question today, we most likely would emphasize the boundaries—love as a responsibility. Our

conversation would affirm the fact that loving Christ is the most important issue in our relationship with Him. In His earliest revelation, God
told the Israelites, "Love the LORD your God with all your heart and
with all your soul and with all your strength" (Deut. 6:5). We would
underscore that this is not an option but a command . . . and our primary responsibility in the relationship.

To stress the importance of this responsibility, we would note
Jesus' answer when the religious lawyer asked Him which of the commandments is the greatest (Matt. 22:34–40). Jesus replied that God's
first and foremost expectation is that we should love Him with the totality of our being. The fact that Jesus used the Greek word *agape* to
describe this love means He is looking for a love that is grounded in
choice and not emotion, a love capable of performing in spite of how
we feel. And since this love is a choice, we will be held responsible for
whether we have chosen to love Him.

Our discussion would also have to include Jesus' last conversation with Peter. Jesus asked Peter three times whether or not he loved
Him, which clearly demonstrates that our love for Christ is of primary
importance to Him. Indeed, we would note that loving Christ is so
important that He has promised a crown reward "to those who love him"
(James 1:12). And we would note that Scripture describes our love for
Him in terms such as yieldedness, sacrifice, surrender, and obedience.

Having tackled the challenge of defining our love for Christ so
thoroughly, we would no doubt feel quite satisfied to have theologized
and biblicized our way through the issue. But we are not really done
yet. I am embarrassed to admit that for years I have taught that loving
Christ is simply about the surrender of our will. As children of the
Enlightenment we find great pleasure in rationally analyzing and defining our way through life. Yet, if we are not careful, we leave little room
for the intangible mysteries and nuances that can fill us with the beauty
of the depth and breadth of love as a living experience.

I agree with John Calvin, who insisted that truth about God is
not merely intended to "flit about in our brains," but to touch our affec-

tions as well. For me, the joy of loving Martie is not in knowing the definitions and the importance of my love for her, but in the experience of my relationship with her as a person.

*For the forgiven woman, loving Jesus was more
than a duty; it was an expression of devotion.*

BEYOND THE BOUNDARIES

If the forgiven woman who poured out her love at the feet of Jesus were to pull up a chair and join our conversation with the seminarian, she no doubt would nod her head in agreement with all that we said about loving Christ—but she would not be satisfied with such a one-sided perspective. She would want to take us beyond our analysis of love as a *responsibility* to the significance of love as a *response*. For her, loving Jesus was more than a duty; it was an expression of devotion. She would tell us of a love that is stimulated by a deep sense of awe, affection, and adoration; of a love that is willing to do risky and radical things if necessary to express a heart of unquenchable gratitude; of gratitude for the fact that although she had lived all of her life with the burden of her sin, yet now she is free and has found someone who truly cares for her and is the liberator of her soul. She would tell us in no uncertain terms that, for her, loving Jesus is more than an item on her list of what she ought to do, but rather a matter of what she wants to do. She would have spoken with an intensity and passion not found in the rather cerebral analysis that we "Bibleboomers" often bring to the discussion.

I wonder whether the difference between this woman's heartfelt love and our more studied relationship to Christ stems from the fact that we don't feel that we have been forgiven much. Is the root of our dilemma that we see ourselves as basically good people? Is it that our relationship with Christ has not been fashioned from the sludge of life because we have met Him on a higher plane? If that is our view, then sharing space with this woman at Jesus' feet will be a difficult challenge.

My dad grew up on a farm in south central Michigan. His boyhood was all about the hard, dirty work of walking the plow behind two workhorses, clearing the forest of trees and the fields of rocks. The St. Joe River, as they affectionately called it, was his source of recreation. He fished from its banks and swam in it in the buff on hot summer days.

Dad was also the first member of his family to go to college, which was a big deal since no one from the time that our family helped pioneer that area of Michigan had even considered it an option. What most of the Stowell clan didn't realize is that the day Dad left for college would be his last day on the farm. God put my dad in other fields—fields of men and women whom he would lead to Christ and shepherd as a faithful pastor.

But as the adage goes, You can take the boy out of the country, but you can't take the country out of the boy. Dad loved his garden. During my childhood our home was on a large tract of land lined by beautiful gardens with dozens of varieties of perennials and his favorite rosebushes. He spent much of his leisure time tending and grooming his little Eden. It was one of the ways in which he stepped out of the stress of his pastoral work.

I didn't grow up on a farm. I grew up in North Jersey, where work was having a paper route to make a little extra money and play was with a ball, bat, and glove with buddies at the park. My Dad's love of gardening periodically led to a collision of interests.

Often—too often for me—my dad would tell me that I needed to spend part of my Saturday with him in the garden. Weeding needed to be done. The flowers had to be deadheaded. There was edging to do and that ever-present purgatory of digging the dandelions out of the lawn. I must say that I usually complied—as though I had a choice—but rarely with a willing spirit. It became particularly painful when my friends would ride by on their bikes on the way to the park while I was working in the yard.

But today I would give anything to have those days back again. Now that I am older, I have a far deeper understanding of the significance of my father in my life. I owe so much to him. If I could go back, I would gladly serve with him in the garden, not from the drudgery of duty, but from a heart of devotion. I would even want to get up early and have him find me already at work. From my perspective today, weeding would be a great way to say to my dad, "Thanks for all you have done. I love you!" And Dad would clearly know that I loved him in more ways than words and cards on Father's Day.

So it is with Christ. As important as the definitions and dogmas are, loving Christ is richer by far than simply coming to grips with the mechanics that describe our love for Him. If our love is to be true and transforming even in the toughest of times, it must be a responsibility that we fulfill as a *response* to His amazing love and marvelous grace that has been poured out in our lives. This is exactly what John has in mind when he writes, "We love because he first loved us" (1 John 4:19).

We are prone to live out our Christianity at the margins, wanting or wishing we could be free to play at life as others do.

DUTY OR DEVOTION?

It seems to me that much of what we do for God arises out of a sense of obligation and duty. Being good is the way we are supposed to be, so we conform. We are prone to live out our Christianity at the margins, wanting or wishing we could be free to play at life as others do. We curiously envy the unrestrained pleasure that we see in those who love themselves, but we nevertheless stay in the yard to do the tasks our Father has given us. Worse yet, some of us have run from the yard of His love to head for the park where we can play the games we want to play and fashion life after our own dreams and desires. And all the while we feel entitled to the benefits of being His child.

It is a mark of growing up spiritually to *want* to do what the Father wants us to do, not out of duty but out of an overriding sense of adoration and devotion. Maturity is measured in our lives when we are gripped with the astounding reality of God's mercy and grace that we gladly serve Him regardless of the toil or denial involved. Authentic Christianity is developing an adoring gratitude that transforms our lives with unquenchable love for Him. True love—love that is tracking toward the bull's-eye—is a response to our devotion to our Father.

Love as a response has a wonderful way of transforming our attitudes and behavior.

THE POWER OF RESPONSIVE LOVE

Love as a response has a wonderful way of transforming our attitudes and behavior. It produces a higher love that escapes mere duty and resonates with a sense of spontaneous expression. I am reminded of the song we used to sing in church when I was a boy:

> After all He's done for me,
> how can I do less than give Him my best
> and live for Him completely,
> after all He's done for me.

Unfortunately, we have been schooled to believe that being good and doing good are enough for Christ. Behavior and love for Him are not often linked in our minds. Even when we do loving things, we would have to admit, if we are honest with ourselves, that on occasion we do them selfishly, for recognition, exchange, or honor.

Early in life the importance of "being good" was engrained into my psyche. I would be a wealthy man today if I had gotten a five-dollar bill every time someone said to me, "You're the pastor's son. You have to be good. You are an example to the other children." I didn't want to be an example . . . I was only five. I wanted to do all the mischievous things my friends were doing.

As adults we may feel that same tension. We feel that we have to be good. After all, we're God's kids and the world is watching. We have been taught that we should "be good" so that we don't disappoint our parents, don't get caught, won't suffer the consequences, won't appear to be hypocrites, don't ruin the reputation of Christ, and so the list goes on. And while these are the damaging downsides of living life on our own terms, Christ-lovers know that these are not the best reasons to be good. If these are our only motivation, we will fail to be strong when we think we won't get caught or we think we can be clever enough to dodge the consequences. The right reason to do good springs from the fact that we are in a relationship—a love relationship with Christ. We love Him for His sake whether or not there would ever be damaging results of self-willed choices.

It is clear that David understood that all of life is about a relationship with the Creator. After committing adultery with Bathsheba and then arranging the murder of her husband, Uriah, he said brokenly to God, "Against you, you only, have I sinned" (Ps. 51:4). David had been wonderfully blessed by God. From his days in the pasture as a shepherd boy to the days when he hid from King Saul among the hills and caves to the era of his great success as King of Israel, David was a debtor to the amazing grace of God in his life. It was this relationship that he had violated with Bathsheba and Uriah, and that was the point of his sorrow.

Jennifer Horne loved being at college. She had grown up in a good home and lived under the restraints of a normal Christian family. Being at college was her first time to be on her own, and she was determined to enjoy every minute of it and also determined to keep a solid Christian testimony. By the second semester she had fallen in love with a great guy. As their relationship progressed, he started making demands that threatened her sense of moral propriety. All her friends were involved with guys and enjoying their sexual freedom. Jennifer struggled with what her parents would think and with what might happen if she were to become pregnant. She worried about losing her boyfriend, but she never thought about the fact of what this might mean to Christ, who desired her loyal love.

Bob Anderson traveled much of the year for his company. He loved his wife and family deeply. Yet he found on those lonely nights in the hotel room, he was tempted to watch the wrong kind of movies or to log onto the Internet for the thrill of some spicy fare. It troubled him when he thought of his wife and the position that he held at his church. But it never crossed his mind to be concerned about what it said about his love for Christ.

What Jennifer and Bob both failed to realize is that their struggles were more than a test of obedience and being good. These were love tests. Would they love themselves and their own interests, or would they love Christ?

For Bill and Debbie Throckmorton, the toughest challenge of their lives revolved around the thought of forgiving their business partner, who had cheated them out of their life savings. This partner technically hadn't done anything illegal, just grossly unfair. Bill and Debbie simply could not get past the sense that forgiving him would let him off the hook. It was more than they wanted to do. In fact, their anger and resentment often felt good to them; it seemed therapeutic in a strange sort of way. Friends understood and even said they would feel the same way. For the Throckmortons, who were good, upstanding church people, forgiveness seemed to be an unreasonable requirement. They never thought of forgiving their offender to please Christ as a statement of their love for Him.

Barbara Miller understands. She is a busy homemaker, shuttling kids, packing lunches, keeping the house clean, cooking at home to save money, and basically extending her life far past normal levels of energy and strength. Most of her friends work outside their homes, and when they got together in those rare getaway moments for Barbara, they would fill the conversation with how they loved their jobs and the diversity and challenge those jobs provided for them. While they never actually said it, Barb always thought they felt sorry for her and looked down on her for having to stay home. She was a gifted and capable person and, in her worst moments, thought that, given the chance, she could outdo any of them in the marketplace.

Barb and her husband had talked this over on several occasions. He felt that since he made enough money for them to live on, it was better for the children to have someone at home with them and that someday they would reap the rewards of her sacrifice. She agreed and decided to stay home. Her decision was also grounded in her belief that God's Word asked her to complement her husband by graciously cooperating with his leadership. Although he never demanded that she stay at home, she felt best doing what she believed God wanted her to do.

When long days at home got the best of her, Barbara reminded herself that her response to her husband was really a loving response to the Lord. As Ephesians 5:22 says, when a wife responds to her husband in this way, she is actually doing it as though she were doing it "as to the Lord." Her heart was encouraged whenever she thought of staying at home as an expression of her love for Jesus Christ.

THE SIGNIFICANCE OF SELF

It would be easy to think at this point that loving Christ is about trashing self. After all, isn't self the real enemy? Actually, Jesus teaches us in Matthew 22:37 that self is a valuable player in the enterprise of loving Him. When an expert in the law asked, "Teacher, which is the greatest commandment in the Law?" Jesus replied, "Love the Lord your God with all your heart and with all your soul and with all your mind." He was saying that "self" is the gift we give to Him. It is the gift He wants. It is the gift that finally proves we love Him.

Self becomes a dirty commodity to be despised only when we keep it for ourselves and love it more than we love God. Self is not the problem. It is the love of self that stands in the way of loving Christ. In fact, no one can love self and love Christ. We can't have it both ways.

We are not talking about the normal and, in fact, healthy love of self that wants to care and provide for our well-being and get enough food and sleep for our essential needs. The sin is to live for self, even serve Christ for self, and yield to the lesser instincts of bringing pleasure to self when in the process of self-fulfillment we become disloyal to Christ.

Those of us who would rather hold on to self need to know that self spent on self is ultimately a hollow, if not destructive, way to spend a life.

> *Those of us who would rather hold on to self need to know that self spent on self is ultimately a hollow, if not destructive, way to spend a life.*

During a two-year imprisonment late in his life, the great British playwright Oscar Wilde wrote a long letter to his homosexual lover—for whom he had left a wife and two children—about the consequences when self is spent on self.

> The gods had given me almost everything. But I let myself be lured into long spells of senseless and sensual ease. . . . I surrounded myself with the smaller natures and the meaner minds. I became the spendthrift of my own genius, and to waste an eternal youth gave me a curious joy. Tired of being on the heights, I deliberately went to the depths in the search for new sensation. . . . Desire, at the end, was a malady, or a madness, or both. I grew careless of the lives of others. I took pleasure where it pleased me, and passed on. I forgot that every little action of the common day makes or unmakes character, and that therefore what one has done in the secret chamber one has some day to cry aloud on the housetop. I ceased to be lord over myself. I was no longer the captain of my soul, and I did not know it. I allowed pleasure to dominate me. I ended in horrible disgrace.[1]

We should not be surprised that loving Christ is about giving all of self to Him. The greatest complaint I heard from wives when I was a pastor was that they felt they were secondary to their husbands' jobs, sports, TV time, and the evening newspaper. Something about true love makes us want to know where we stand in a relationship. If the one we love loves something else more—oneself or desire or possessions— then we feel that we are not really loved after all.

If we claim that we love Christ, He wants to know where He stands among all the stuff of our lives. Is He the compelling priority, or just one thing among the many things that get a little attention here and a little attention there?

What constitutes true love for Christ? It is an unflinching commitment to yield the totality of myself to His will, wishes, and interests. But most importantly, it is a commitment driven and defined by my response to the marvelous gift of grace that He has generously showered on my life. By far, the best thing to do with self and with all that self possesses is to give it away as a grateful gift of love. When that happens, the transforming power of love is fully engaged.

CHOICES OF THE HEART

Life is full of choices. But for the follower of Christ, they are all inevitably love choices that affect the most profound relationship that we possess. Do we love a particular temptation or the thrill of some private sin more than we love Him? Do we love the thrill of the kill in the competitive environment of the workplace more than we love Him, even when that competitive drive threatens to take us over the line of integrity? Do we love the security of personal wealth more than we love the advance of His kingdom work? Do we love the future on our own terms more than we love what He might do through us if we willingly placed our future in His hands?

If Christ asks for our children in His service, can He have them? If He asks us to serve Him in some humble unseen way, will we be available? If He leads through suffering and the loss of comfort, do we love Him enough to take up our cross and follow without an "attitude"?

Our love for Christ is revealed in the trenches of life,
not in the pew or the pulpit.

Our love for Christ is revealed in the trenches of life, not in the pew or the pulpit. This truth guarantees that our choices will often be more complex than simple and more demanding than convenient. Loving Christ will often be in contention with the power players of our culture: money, material gain, sensual seductions, position, power, and self-interest. But when we see the choices as a decision between the value of Christ and the value of the competitors, the decision becomes clearer. Ultimately, the choices we make stand as the ultimate judge of the sincerity of our love.

Christ doesn't just want our heads or the sterile surrender of a will that has been cajoled, frightened, codified, or simply required to obey Him. He isn't impressed with our works if they are done only out of ritual or obligation. To the hardened hearts of the religious folk of His day, He said, "You hypocrites! Isaiah was right when he prophesied about you: 'These people honor me with their lips, but their hearts are far from me'" (Matt. 15:7–8).

Christ wants our affection. He wants the adoration of our hearts. He finds pleasure in followers who join the woman at His feet.

The belief that we must buck up and love Jesus and that external patterns of behavior prove our love and loyalty to Christ is a treacherous pursuit. When we adopt this attitude, something bad happens on the inside. As we master codes of conduct, we are victimized by pride and forget that the real issues of life are defined by what is in our hearts.

In my first pastorate, a colleague of mine led a large and growing church and was easily—in the best sense of the word—the envy of most other pastors. He held high denominational offices and was sought after nationally as a preacher and consultant on church growth. External signals of godliness were the mark of his trade. The kind of haircuts men had, the kind of clothes women wore, one's demeanor and behavior in church, the kind of music played and listened to, the entertainment people enjoyed—these were the hallmarks for his ministry. Once during a statewide meeting he leaned over and said to me, "You know, Joe, your hair is too long to be able to sing in my choir!" Actually, there were probably some better reasons that I couldn't sing in his church choir, but I just smiled and said, "Oh really?"

Sometime later, to our shock and great disappointment, we learned that this pastor had abandoned his church and family and had gone to the south to live with a woman he had been counseling. We were astonished at this behavior, given how strict he was about so many things. But had we understood, we might have guessed. The externals had become the playing field of his relationship to Christ, and the inner world of Christ's desires and dreams was left unprotected. This man's love for Christ had become a responsibility expressed in outward conformity. All of us who know him rejoice today that he and his wife have been reconciled and that, as he himself would tell you, he understands the treachery of an externalized spirituality. He now knows that a true love for Christ is not just a responsibility but a response that consumes all of one's heart, soul, and strength.

I am reminded of the wisdom of the writer of the Proverbs who said, "Above all else, guard your heart, for it is the wellspring of life" (Prov. 4:23). Love as a responsibility is about lifestyle. Love as a response is about heartstyle. God is not interested in our lifestyle if it does not begin with heartstyle. From God's perspective, lifestyle without heartstyle is no style at all.

CHAPTER THREE

ASPECTS OF LOVE

Learning Love at the Feet of Jesus

I remember traveling through the south as a child on family vacations and noticing drinking fountains, restrooms, and restaurants designated as "whites only" and "coloreds only." At this early stage in my life, to this "white boy" from the north, it was little more than a cultural peculiarity. But I have come now to understand that if you were "colored," it meant far more than having dark skin. It was an offense of the deepest kind. And you felt the blow every time you had to publicly bow to a cultural statement of your unworthiness by using a segregated facility. Riding buses was no better. Blacks sat in the back, and if the bus was full, you always gave up your seat to a white person. Until, that is, Rosa Parks refused to yield her seat and ignited the civil rights movement that freed blacks from the "whites-only" rules and a host of other injustices.

To African-Americans everywhere, Rosa Parks became a hero. She had done what they always wanted to do. Her courage to take a stand for justice and her people struck an immediate cord of identity. Her willingness to stand—or sit, as was the case for her—in the face of an oppressive system has made her a legend. Every black baby who has been bounced on grandma's knee has heard the story enough times to recite it by heart. Justly so, millions still find personal hope and courage in the telling of Rosa Park's noble deed.

For Christians of the first century, there is little doubt that the moving story of the sinful woman at the feet of Jesus created a similar point of identity. Her adoring devotion to Jesus in the face of great hostility and rejection became a defining metaphor for their own lives. Early Christians were called to exercise their faith amid life-threatening ridicule and rejection from both the secular and religious world of their day. It is easy to see why this obscure, tainted woman who dauntlessly expressed her love to Jesus in the dining room of Simon the Pharisee became a ready-made hero.

Although two thousand years removed, you would think that the legacy of this heroine would still carry clout in our hearts. But she is often a forgotten feature on the New Testament play list. Or, at best, she gets second billing to stories like those of the Prodigal Son and the Good Samaritan. Yet her story is more our story than theirs are. If we had the smallest glimpse of the depth and breadth of the gift of Christ's love for us, we would be jealous of the fact that she did what we wish we could do at Jesus' feet.

Like the woman, we owe much to Christ. He has expended His amazing grace to liberate us from the debilitating grasp of sin and hell. And as though that weren't enough, He is the unfailing provider of a thousand graces every day. He is our advocate and defender in the midst of the oppressors of our lives. As Romans 12 assures us, our Lord faithfully takes up our cause against offenders, which frees us to love them in spite of the blows they inflict on us. Christ fights for us in the high places where spiritual warfare is waged against us. When Satan accuses us before the throne of the Father, He defends us. He alone provides security and confidence in an increasingly hostile environment. He is our helper and friend. And lest we forget, it cost Him His life to make all this possible.

Just thinking of these inexplicable blessings makes my heart wish that I, like the woman, could break out of a crowd and run to Jesus, honoring Him with the very best gifts of worshipful adoration I could bring. What a thrill it would be to sense the hush of the clamor and hear His voice rise to affirm and defend my love for Him! To hear Him silence my enemies would comfort my heart. What a joy to know the peace of resting at His feet! To feel assured that because of Him everything in my life is finally okay would only make me want to love Him more.

All of this actually happens every day in our lives. It doesn't happen just in Simon's house. Our gifts of active, adoring love fall like tears on His feet and perfume His presence with an aroma that delights everyone around. Even though we can't hear Him or see Him, He never leaves us nor forsakes us. His protecting, defending work is forever engaged. Therefore on that glad day when we see Him face-to-face, we will not be able to contain ourselves. We will run to His feet and gratefully adore Him . . . forever!

For all this and more, our hearts should passionately search for ways to show Him how much we love Him now. But how can we love Him? Is it really possible to touch the Divine with a love language that He will understand?

Going to school on the woman's story is a good place to begin. In her we find not only a hero with whom we readily identify but also a powerful picture of the kind of love that Christ accepts and affirms. In that brief encounter at Simon's table a whole array of loving qualities poured from her heart. If we wonder how we as mere mortals could ever touch the heart of the Divine with effective love, she shows us the way.

LET ME COUNT THE WAYS

Our heroine's bold demonstration of love creates a compelling and challenging pattern that mentors our love for Christ. I am reminded of Elizabeth Barrett Browning's poem, "How Do I Love Thee? Let Me Count the Ways." The ways this woman expressed her adoring affection to Jesus were many. More importantly, Jesus affirmed them as the kind of love that connected with His heart.

We should not assume that our love touches Christ when in reality He doesn't feel loved at all. I often wonder if our ritualized kind of Christianity touches the heart of Christ. Does He know we love Him because we have mastered all the codes and traditions of our faith? Does He know we love Him when we are faithful in the easy times, when there is no sacrifice, when there is no press of the world in our face? Do our secret lives and the coldness of our hearts inform Him that somehow lip service has become the prevailing expression of our love?

One thing is clear: Jesus' appreciation and unhesitating defense of the woman's actions affirm that her kind of love is exactly what He is looking for. If Jesus has a love language, she spoke it.

What is Christ's love language? The woman charts a course that all of us can follow.

A WORSHIPING LOVE

When John wrote in 1 John 3:18, "Let us not love with words or tongue but with actions and in truth," he could have used our heroine as a leading example. She was not content merely to talk about her grateful love for Jesus; she acted it out in concrete ways. Indeed, it is instructive to note that she is the only one in the story who says nothing, yet impacts and teaches us most profoundly. The love that touches Christ proves itself in the reality of our everyday behavior in the workplace, in relationships, and in the handling of our possessions. Authentic love is an *active* love. It is her love in action that is so instructive.

> *The love that touches Christ proves itself in the reality of our everyday behavior in the workplace, in relationships, and in the handling of our possessions.*

It is hard to miss the fact that what she is doing is first and foremost an act of adoring *worship*. The core meaning of worship is to express the worth of the one who is being honored. Any thought that Christ feels loved because once or twice a week we show up to *do worship* misses the point that worship is a daily, lifelong expression of the worth and value of Christ in our attitudes and activities. As one person has put it, "When we say, 'we will now begin to worship,' we owe God an apology." For our heroine, Jesus was worth the risk to show up at her accuser's party, worth the embarrassment to step from the crowd and approach Him, worth the price of the valuable perfume, worth serving at His feet with kisses and tears.

The mediocrity of our Christianity becomes nakedly apparent when we stop to consider the last time that we did something radical, risky, or expensive to simply say to Christ, "You are worth it all and more." The greater the risk, the more expensive the gift, the more costly the sacrifice, the lower the level of service, the bigger the statement of worth.

There is no doubt that sacrificing for the one you love speaks loudly about his or her worth and the quality of your love. In Jesus' day, one of the most prized possessions a woman could have was her perfume. Since there were no personal cosmetics, perfume served as their only cover. Perfume was costly, extracted from the oils of plants and flowers. A woman's perfume was her signature, and the best perfume was used only for the most special occasions.

This woman brought her best to Jesus. Nothing would be too costly for her adoration and worship of Him than something she held dear. I am reminded of the words of David when he refused to receive as a gift the threshing floor where he would build an altar to the Lord. His response was, "No, I insist on paying you for it. I will not sacrifice to the LORD my God burnt offerings that cost me nothing" (2 Sam. 24:24).

Just as Jesus was profoundly taken with this woman's active, loving worship, so the perfume of our lives broken unconditionally at His feet will impress Him with the depth and sincerity of our love. Unless, that is, we get ensnared in the glory of our own worthiness as exceptional worshipers. Isn't that the embarrassment of it all—that in seeking to love Him in exceptional ways, we become exceptionally impressed with ourselves? The only remedy is to continually remind ourselves that being counted among the "forgiven much" can never be about us. We aren't even worthy to be forgiven. That is why Christ's love for us is couched in terms like mercy and grace. The slightest twinge of feeling that our loving expressions of His worth should be recognized, celebrated, or at least "thanked" should warn us of a serious heart problem. We will know we are free of self-worship when we are able to love anonymously without regret.

I doubt that the immoral lady of the town where Simon ruled ever gave a second thought as to who would congratulate her for what she had done. Do you think she ceremoniously held the perfume up for all to see its value before she poured it? She certainly didn't stage this event to make her way into the Gospels or to be celebrated through the history of the church as a model of legitimate love. She was driven to express His worth regardless of anything else. It was all about Him and not about her, which is what makes her active worship so pure and acceptable.

She was driven to express His worth regardless of anything else. It was all about Him and not about her.

Furthermore, we should note that this woman had time to think about what she was doing and its ramifications. This was not a spontaneous, knee-jerk reaction to the moment. Her acts of loving worship were *intentional.* When she heard that Jesus was going to be at Simon's house, she made a plan. Not only would she meet Him there, but she would also bring her perfume to anoint Him. Count on it, she knew the risk and measured the cost.

Her actions make me wonder about the last time I intentionally planned to do something to communicate to Christ how much I love Him. Let's see . . . on Sunday I write a check. And while that is part of what He wants from me, it is usually little more than what I have become accustomed to doing. I need to change that. Every check should be a conscious act of loving worship, a statement that I love Him more than all I have, that He is worth more than silver or gold to me.

Too often we are motivated to give so that we might be blessed or out of a sense of duty or to keep a clear conscience. But true giving is about how worthy Christ is. When I intentionally plan my giving in the light of His worthiness, He feels loved and worshiped. Even so, I have to admit that talking about money as a means of worshiping Christ seems shamefully small in light of so many who have given so much more than money—even their lives—out of love for Him.

We should resolve to start each day by asking, "What can I do today to express my adoring love for the worthy Christ?" If you are engaged in life at all, it won't take long to think of a meaningful gift to bring to His feet. Make your plan, then resolve that before the day is out you will have executed the plan. Opportunities to intentionally express your love for Him literally abound at the crossroads of every choice, every thought, every personal interaction, every financial decision. Look for people who are in need, who long to be forgiven, who need encouragement. Plan to avoid temptation and to speak the truth in love. Plot ways to give and to be generous in Jesus' name. Create time with your children and focus your personal resources, energies, and attention on your spouse. Decide that you will not spread gossip or harm another person's reputation. If you are serious about loving Christ, it will be evident in your being managed by the consistent intent of using all of life to send a message to Christ: a message of His worth and our limitless gratitude.

TRANSFORMING LOVE

As she steps from the margins of the dining hall to make her way among the guests, she steals the moment by her very presence. She doesn't have to do anything else but be there and invade the space of the lounging invitees to make a scene. Add the sobbing, her approaching Jesus, and her falling at His feet, and you have a moment that everyone in attendance will never forget. Yet it is what happens next that offends Simon most deeply and threatens Jesus most directly. As she lets down her hair to wipe the tears that wet His feet, you can bet that the crowd gasps with a hushed amazement. For a woman to let her hair down in public was a forbidden act of sensuality; it would be as shocking as a woman going topless in our day.

Interestingly, Jesus does not reprove her. One strains to understand why this open display of an impermissible act of sensuality draws no rebuke from Jesus. Does He perceive that her act is not sensually motivated, but rather is the only way she knows to express love? Often we expect newcomers to the family of faith to know all the proper ways to express their newfound joy. It is striking that Jesus repeatedly seems to be more tolerant than we toward those who seek to do well but don't know better. What we can be sure of is that her intent was in no way sexual or sinful. Had that been the case, Jesus (who has just read Simon's mind) certainly could have discerned her intentions and would have rejected her advances. Whatever is going on is clearly not a temptation to sin—which leaves the question, "What is she doing, and why does Jesus let her do it?"

It fascinates me to think that she is bringing her past ways of living, the tools of her trade, and laying them at Jesus' feet in an act of purifying surrender. Letting down her hair may signal a yielding of her past to Jesus. And the perfume? That is undoubtedly what she used to sweeten her bed for her clients.

This is a transforming love—a love that brings to Jesus everything that has defiled our past and threatens our present purity. Bringing it all to His feet is a living testimony that we no longer need the shameful stuff of our past because our love for Jesus is far more compelling than anything we have loved before.

Bringing it all to His feet is a living testimony that we no longer need the shameful stuff of our past because our love for Jesus is far more compelling than anything we have loved before.

The songwriter catches the spirit of life-transforming love when he writes . . .

All to Jesus I surrender, all to Him I freely give;
I will ever love and trust Him, in His presence daily live. . . .
All to Thee, my blessed Savior, I surrender all.

Love brings it all: all the foul habits of the past, all the pride, all the self-consumption. Without reservation, regardless of who is watching, in spite of what others may say, Christ-lovers lay it all at His feet. He receives it all and removes it as far as the east is from the west. And, by the way, He is not surprised, repulsed, or shocked by what we bring. He has seen and felt it all before—two thousand years ago as He suffered the blows of the very things we now break at His feet.

We shouldn't expect the proud Simon, whose sensitivities are in bondage to unbending traditions, ever to understand this kind of powerful statement. He has just gone through extensive ritualistic cleansing to eat this meal in purity. For this woman to invade the meal is bad enough, but for her to let down her hair and to fill the room with the fragrance that symbolizes her sinful life is more than he could bear. The profound beauty of all of this is that sinners come to Christ just as they are, while the righteous often miss the point because they believe they have no defilement to bring to Him.

I recently received an e-mail message from a listener to our radio broadcast *Proclaim*. He wrote about years of trying to resist the intrigue and seduction of pornographic material on the Internet. To his dismay, nothing seemed to stem his appetite, and his failure to overcome these temptations had defeated him. After listening to a broadcast, he decided to put a picture of Jesus on his computer screen. He remarked that seeing Christ has made him aware of the surpassing value of his relationship with Him. In a sense he brought his struggle to Christ and laid the defeating desire at His feet. He e-mailed me to say he had been free for weeks from his moral failure of the past.

If you love Christ, search the tools that are used to keep you in sin and bring them to Him as presents of repentance. Do you have a passion for sensual fulfillment, the greed of personal gain, a mind that con-

structs fantasies of sin and shame, time wasted in meaningless and sometimes perilous pursuits, or manipulating people for personal advantage? Bring it all to His feet. Ask Him to transform each passion into a
desire that pleases and glorifies Him. Bring your greed to His feet in a
commitment to pursue the gain of His kingdom through generous sac-
rifices of time and resources. Let Him transform your mind to think
His thoughts and devise ways to advance His cause. Place at His feet
the people you have used and abused for your own purposes, committing yourself instead to serve them for their good and gain.

Tom Maharis is pastor of Manhattan Bible Church on New York's
rough north side, but he is no stranger to the streets of a drug-ravaged
culture. He grew up there. He pushed drugs on the streets and helped
to weave treachery and danger into the fabric of the very neighborhoods
where he now serves Christ. Miraculously redeemed from his sin and
devastating lifestyle, Tom has taken all that he knew and loved about
life in the alleys and has broken it at Jesus' feet. He has returned to the
same streets and alleys with the same savvy he used in drug-peddling
and now uses it to the advantage of the good news of Christ. Many of
his old buddies now know Christ and radiate with testimonies that rival
the greatest acts of God's grace.

Tom married his girlfriend, Vicki, and now they minister side by
side. Together they founded the Manhattan Bible Church. If you attend
his church on any given Sunday, you will worship with street people,
former prostitutes, AIDS-infected reformed drug addicts, and executives from Madison Avenue. In a sense his church must be a lot like
heaven because it seems that some from every tribe and nation are there.
Tom took the tools of the trade of his sinful life and uses them to this
day as an expression of love to Christ. In doing so, he shares space with
the sinful woman at Jesus' feet.

COURAGEOUS LOVE

The most obvious aspect of the woman's love is that it is *courageous.* She couldn't have chosen a more hostile forum in which to express

her love to Jesus. It is the religious crowd under the direction of their fearless leader Simon who most despise the sinners of the streets. To enter Simon's house, let alone his dining area, is to love Jesus in the face of supreme ridicule and rejection. But her love for Jesus is so profound that it is able to thrive regardless of the nature of the crowd. The focus of its energy doesn't care who is there, what people say, who is watching, or who thinks less of her for it.

> *The most obvious element of the woman's love is that it is courageous. She couldn't have chosen a more hostile forum in which to express her love to Jesus.*

I love the way her courage enabled her to be vulnerable. Many of us have loved and in so doing have opened ourselves up to being hurt by the one we love. We have said that we will never love again. The question is whether we can become vulnerable again. Are we willing to open up once more because we love Christ? Can we trust Him to protect, defend, and reward our love for Him? Do we love Him enough to be willing to be taken advantage of for His sake? Misunderstood for His sake? Abandoned for His sake? After all, we need to remember that He was willing to love us with that kind of courageous, self-denying resolve all the way to the cross.

When Mother Teresa addressed the National Prayer Breakfast in Washington, Vice President Al Gore and his wife were seated to her right and, on the other side of the podium, sat President Bill Clinton and his wife. There, in the presence of powerful people who support the cause of abortion, Mother Teresa said,

> I feel that the greatest destroyer of peace today is abortion, because it is war against the child, a direct killing of the innocent child, murder by the mother herself. . . . By abortion the mother does not learn to love, but kills even her own

child to solve her problems. And by abortion the father is told that he does not have to take any responsibility at all for the child he has brought into the world. That father is likely to put other women into the same trouble. So abortion just leads to more abortion. Any country that accepts abortion is not teaching its people to love, but to use violence to get what they want. This is why the greatest destroyer of love and peace is abortion.

The crowd rose to its feet in thunderous applause while the Clintons and the Gores sat awkwardly waiting for the program to continue.

This frail, little, powerless woman exemplified a vulnerable courage to do and say what is right regardless of the crowd or the intimidation of the most powerful people in the world. It is that kind of risky courage that lovers of Christ are willing to display when it is necessary.

We all find it easy to affirm our commitment to Christ within the safe confines of church or a small-group Bible study. But eventually our loyalty must be expressed in the hostile arenas of the workplace, in the face of an offender who needs to be forgiven, or for some of us, in the presence of a spouse who doesn't share our commitment to Christ. Or do friends intimidate our resolve to live in a loving way toward Him?

It might even be that our Christian friends—that religious crowd again—do not understand or appreciate the radical and risky nature of our love decisions. A woman I was counseling—a woman who was struggling to forgive her husband for deep offenses—told me that her biggest problem was her Christian friends who were telling her she was "crazy" to extend grace and mercy to him. Their advice? "Kick the bum out!" Christ-lovers don't care what anyone says or thinks. They love Christ, and that is the most important reality in their lives.

The woman's act of love is, in the context of this evening, indeed a risky thing. It is as though she says in her heart, "I don't care who's there, what they say, or what they do. I must tell Jesus how much I love Him." And she so willingly and without intimidation expresses her love in the face of traditionally accepted norms and expectations—codes that would have said you cannot love Jesus like this. But she knows, unlike the rigidly programmed Simon, that love often flies in the face of self-imposed restrictions, and that she is more in tune with the heart of Jesus than a hypocritical Pharisee. When you put yourself at risk to love Him, remember that He will be your defender and advocate. Perhaps He will not always show Himself in immediate or visible ways, but He will be there, protecting, bestowing grace, and using your love for Him to bring about His ultimate, wise design.

ADVOCATING LOVE

As she stands in the crowd gathered around the dining room, it quickly becomes apparent to her that Jesus has been rudely slighted by Simon. Undoubtedly, He is the only one who did not have His feet washed, the only guest not to be greeted with a kiss. Didn't Simon know that his special guest of the evening deserves to be honored with an anointing? Sensing the shame and embarrassment of this insult, she breaks from the crowd to rush to Jesus. Bursting into tears, she washes His feet. She can offer the kiss He was refused; the anointing of the guest of honor will become her privilege. If no one else will stick up for Christ, she will. Her love for Him refuses to let her stand by while others discount His worth and, worse yet, defame Him with this calculated snub. Her love will be an advocating love. She will be His advocate in the face of ridicule and insult.

Martie and I were enjoying some uniquely Chicago-style pasta dishes in an Italian diner one evening and enjoying a conversation with our server. She told us she was going on a trip to an Asian country with a friend to discover the teachings of a guru who would bring her, as she put it, healing and purpose. We listened further as she talked about other aspects of her trip. As Martie and I walked home, my heart was burning with conviction. Christ was the answer to her search, and I had not been His advocate among false gods. I was so engaged in the conversation and so taken with the details of her trip that I failed to think of turning her face toward the one I love. It was a low point in my desire to develop a loving relationship with Christ. I failed as His advocate.

I recently received a letter from a man in New York City telling me of a play about to open that blasphemes Christ in most shameful and degrading ways. In the play, titled *Corpus Christi,* Jesus is openly portrayed as a reckless homosexual who has had random and frequent affairs with His disciples. The play delves into other equally graphic and gross distortions of the biblical account of Jesus' life.

The letter included a plea to write to my congressman to urge cutting off the federal funding being supplied for this play through the National Endowment for the Arts. It was a clear moment of advocacy for Christ. To his dismay, the letter writer was not finding much support for his endeavor.

I have always been somewhat amazed by the tolerance Christians seem to have for using the Lord's name in vain in public. Most wince with disgust at the so-called four-letter words of vulgarity, yet they rarely blink an eye at the way Christ's name is used in expletives of anger or disgust.

Loving Christ is about coming to His defense in a world that at best grants Him no honor and at worst distorts and defames His name.

If anyone spoke against my wife or children—the people I love most—I would not hesitate for a moment to come to their defense. Loving Christ is about coming to His defense in a world that at best grants Him no honor and at worst distorts and defames His name. Christ-lovers need not be obnoxious in this defense but can find appropriate ways to become effective advocates for His name and reputation.

A PERSONAL LOVE

In all of this it is important to note that this woman's love is intensely personal. She had chosen a life of sin, and Jesus alone has offered her the solution to her heart's deepest ache. He—and no one else—has offered her acceptance in a community where she has been pushed to the edges and offered no hope. He has become her advocate in a setting where no one else would dare take her side. This redemptive relationship depends on and needs no one but Jesus. She feels no obligation to seek others for approval. She has no need to clear her actions with others who may or may not understand. She has been loved in a most personal way, and she will do what is right for Jesus.

In the end, our love for Christ must be free from the restraints and constraints of the pressures and perspectives of others. Our love for Him is, in the best sense of the term, no one else's business. We love Him because He first loved us. It's that simple. It's that personal.

This truth in turn renders our love wonderfully real. As we have noted, the incident in Simon's house is not a staged event. The woman has no idea that she will go down in history as a celebrity among those who seek to love Christ. This is not an orchestrated worship experience, well planned to get in her enemy's face. There is something simple and wonderful about her love. It is *refreshingly real*. It arises from the depth of her soul. It is so demanding that she cannot suppress the desire to demonstrate her love. There is nothing plastic here. This is authentic love, and it leads our hearts on a search to be moved so deeply as well.

LIFE AT JESUS' FEET

It takes the sinful woman to teach us that life is best lived—most appropriately lived—at Jesus' feet. While it was appropriate for a guest's feet to be washed, it would usually be the cheek that is kissed and the head that is anointed. It seems evident that for her to kiss Jesus' cheek and to anoint His head would be too bold and assuming. She is so struck with His greatness and the unusual gift of His grace to someone like her that she sheds the gifts of her love at His feet. No doubt feeling unworthy, she kneels where the servant assigned to Jesus would have stood. Her love and repentance drive her to posture herself at His feet in humble service to Him. There is nothing presumptuous here, no thought that she is His equal. She hardly deserves to be in His presence, so she comes as His servant. She demonstrates that true love is a humble, unassuming love.

It takes the sinful woman to teach us that life is best lived—most appropriately lived—at Jesus' feet.

In your love for Christ, have you ever assumed that you are doing Him a favor, and that, after all, He is quite blessed to have you loving Him? Have you ever served in a position to be noticed or to leverage power? Must you be an elder, or would you be content to tell Christ how much you love Him by serving as an usher, a nursery worker, or a volunteer who picks up the sanctuary, sweeps the floors, and cleans the bathrooms after everyone else is gone?

The image of living out our lives at Jesus' feet has many points of reference. John the Baptist was so taken by the transcendent worth of Christ that he felt unworthy to even kneel at His feet to untie His shoe (Luke 3:16). Mary sat at Jesus' feet to listen and worship in contrast to her sister, who was too busy doing good deeds (Luke 10:38–42). Jesus commended Mary for choosing the better thing, but this despairing woman, humbly bowing at Jesus' feet, teaches us most clearly about a heart that loves much. Her pattern must be the measure of our loving aspirations toward Christ.

Check the profile. Can you think of the last time you actively worshiped Christ in an intentional act of love that cost you something? Have you ever brought to Him the tools of your sinful ways and, in an expression of personal transformation, broken them at his feet? Have you loved Him recently with courage in the face of intimidating circumstances? Is your love strong enough to be willing to become vulnerable for Him? When was the last time you took the opportunity to express your love by taking up His cause as an advocate of His name? Have you ever loved Him in radical and risky ways, or have you colored your religion well within the lines of comfort and convenience? Would those who observe your life regularly say that they see your love for Christ because you humbly serve Him in a personal way that reflects a reality that drives your soul?

Overwhelmed? Don't be. We grow in our love for Him. This is not about perfect love. That is what He gave to us. This is about authentically progressing in love. My love for my wife is far more comprehensive and instinctive than it was thirty-four years ago. I loved her then, and I love her now. But my love grows deeper and better with time.

Lest you think that all of this is too much to master, the good news is that this is not a project to be mastered. It is a passion to be expressed. As we seek to love Christ, these aspects of the woman's love will instinctively flow from our lives. Our heroine didn't check the list in her pocket to make sure she covered all the points in her adoring gestures of love. She simply seized the opportunity, and He loved and defended her for it.

Her profile of effective love challenges me. It sets a high mark that provides a target to shoot for. But I must admit that as much as her love challenges me, Simon's attitude convicts me. If I asked you whether your life most resembles the woman's or Simon's, you would want to say the woman's. We like to think of ourselves as being with her at Jesus' feet. Yet, upon examination, we might find that most of our lives are far closer to the standoffish, self-righteous Pharisee, whom Christ reproved. A glimpse of Simon's attitudes and the reason for them may help to explain why we find it so hard to consistently express an authentic love for Christ.

CHAPTER FOUR

SIMONIZED SAINTS

Symptoms of a Loveless Life

Art was his life. He had plenty of money and circled the globe to collect the very best. His more than adequate house was filled with Monets, Picassos, and many of the world's finest treasures. But after years of having it all, he found his world shattered when cancer took his wife. To memorialize his love for her, he decided to gather an even better collection in her honor.

The collector's love became focused on his son. They did everything together, and he took pride in all that his son accomplished. It was a sad day when his son went off to fight in the Vietnam War. But not as sad as the day when the news came that his son had been killed in battle. He was crushed. He lost all interest in collecting. His life was reduced to lonely memories of days gone by with those he loved.

Years later, a knock at his door found him standing face-to-face with a rather common, slightly tattered person who was holding a picture under his arm. The visitor told the collector that he had been his son's best friend in Vietnam and now made a living as a street painter. He explained that while he was in Vietnam he had painted a picture of his friend and wanted to know if the father might be interested in it. The old man took the picture in his hands and immediately noticed the clear resemblance. The sparkle in his son's eyes brought back a flood of memories. No one would have said that it was great art, but he took the picture tearfully and gratefully. He immediately hung it above the mantel where his favorite picture had hung since before his wife had died.

When the old man passed away, his entire collection went to the most prestigious auction house in London. Needless to say, this created quite a stir among museum curators and wealthy people from around the world. On the day of the auction the room was crowded with the who's who of collecting. The gavel sounded as the hushed crowd that jammed the auction house watched the first picture being unveiled. To everyone's astonishment, it was the picture that the street painter had given to the old collector. The auctioneer waited for a bid. No one moved. He explained that this was a picture of the collector's son who was killed in Vietnam. As the crowd grew restless, the auctioneer explained that the instructions in the will required that this picture be auctioned first.

Finally, to get the bidding started, the auctioneer offered the painting for fifty dollars. Still no one responded—until a voice came from the back of the room from a man who said he was that soldier's friend and, in fact, the painter of the picture. He said he would bid the fifty dollars to get the picture back. The auctioneer called for other bids and, hearing none, gaveled the bids closed as the crowd settled in for the real action.

But to everyone's surprise, the auctioneer gaveled the auction closed. The crowd protested in disbelief. To which the auctioneer replied, "It's in the old man's will: 'Whoever takes the son gets it all'!"

We can say the same thing: "Whoever takes the Son gets it all." When we take Jesus, God's Son, as Savior, it is the Father's will that we receive all the spiritual riches of our inheritance in Him. Grace provides everything we need for life and eternity. Once we are touched with the undeserved love of Christ, life ceases to be about collecting the masterpieces of our own accomplishments. It is about the Son and a grateful devotion to Him. The apostle Paul expressed it this way, that he counted all things loss and his very best achievements like waste so that he could know the unsurpassed grace of Christ in his life (Phil. 3:7–8). For Christ-lovers, life is not about us and our accomplishments, but about living to adore Him.

SELF-ADORATION OR GOD-CENTERED DEVOTION?

The great artist Michelangelo produced some of the best works of art the world has ever seen. His sculpture of David and the multiple paintings on the ceiling of the Sistine Chapel are among the greatest creations of all time. Nearly all of his subject matter was religious, and he often worked at the bidding of the pope. Since he was a devout man, we should not be surprised that he took appropriate pride in what he was doing for God.

Toward the end of his life, under the influence of his dear friend, Vittoria Colonna, he became intrigued with what the Reformers were teaching about justification through faith apart from works. Accepting the reality that all of his good works could do nothing to remove his sin, he embraced Christ as his forgiving Savior. This act changed everything for him. Michelangelo now realized that what he had supposedly done to gain favor with God had actually eclipsed God in his life. In a sonnet penned in his later years he confessed,

> . . . Whence the loving fancy that made of art
>   my idol and my king,
> I know now well that it was full of wrong. . . .
> Painting and sculpture shall no longer calm
>   the soul turned to that love divine
> that spread its arms on the cross to take us in.

As taken as he was with Christ, Michelangelo never stopped expressing himself through art. He was busy until the day he died. But he did it then for a different reason than in the past—not for merit, but for love. One writer observes,

> Michelangelo worked down to the end. . . . Nonetheless, the
> change was a radical one: art, which had become the primary

interest, the "idol and king" of his life, now becomes a means to serve God humbly.[1]

Michelangelo was overwhelmed with the touch of redemption and never recovered from the encounter.

Simon the Pharisee never made this turn. In fact, he would have been shocked to think that his life did not please God. What is troubling is that his good behavior and lack of love for Christ may give us a clue about ourselves—if we are willing to see ourselves in the mirror of his well-intentioned but deeply flawed attitudes and reactions.

But then, seeing ourselves as we really are is a difficult assignment. We rationalize and excuse our weaknesses and sins. We quickly forget the conviction of the Word. We resist the accurate criticisms of spouse and friends. We tend to wrap our lives in a shroud of self-deceit that keeps us feeling quite good about ourselves.

We have all seen people on beaches and in other public places whose garb looks strange, and we wonder whether they have looked in the mirror that morning. After sitting in church behind a lady in an outrageous hat, Robert Burns, the Scottish poet, couldn't resist writing,

> Would to God the gift to give us
> To see ourselves as others see us.

Martie had been after me for months about my putting on weight, and I, quite frankly, didn't get it. I felt fine, ate well, and slept well, and my friends still liked me—so what was the big deal? The big deal was stepping out of the shower one day and catching a glance of my true condition in the mirror. That reality check made me admit that Martie had a point. If I had any self-respect, I needed to change my life habits.

Simon is a mirror. We may not see ourselves as the exact replica of his image, but his self-absorbed response to Christ may very well tell the story of why we live blindly on in our own loveless rituals and religious habits.

AN UNUSUAL DINNER GUEST

I find myself wondering why Simon would have invited Jesus to dinner in the first place. As a Pharisee Simon was certainly aware of how popular Jesus had become with the masses, and he would have been deeply disturbed by Jesus' disruptive and dangerous teaching. The large following that Jesus was generating threatened the power base of religious leaders like Simon. In addition, the freshness of the truth that Jesus taught left Simon's oppressive codes and traditions sounding stuffy and bureaucratic.

The news that Jesus was coming to town would not have made Simon's day. As the local religious expert, for him to ignore such a popular person as Jesus would have been a political mistake. Jesus' credentials as a teacher were unparalleled. Everywhere He went, He attracted crowds. The reports of His miracles had authenticated His claims. For Jesus to be coming his way was a big occasion for the town—and a big problem for Simon. No doubt he lost some sleep over the ramifications of Jesus' visit.

Simon had a lot to lose from Jesus' intrusion. Unfortunately, his entrenched perspectives didn't permit him to recognize that it also meant he had Christ to gain.

Most troubling were the potential ramifications for Simon personally. The problem with opening our lives fully to Christ is that He tends to threaten the control and comfort of our well-ordered existence, and that was the case with Simon. If the townspeople were to adopt the teachings of Jesus and turn their hearts to follow Him, much of Simon's teaching would be discredited, his power and influence would diminish, and his hypocrisy and oppressive policies would be exposed. He had a lot to lose from Jesus' intrusion into his domain. Unfortunately, his entrenched perspectives didn't permit him to recognize that it also meant he had Christ to gain. He had no connection to the reality that all loss in the face of winning Christ is no loss at all.

In light of these dynamics, the fact that he invited Jesus to dinner cannot go unnoticed. To eat with someone in those days was a symbol of friendship and social acceptance. That is why the Pharisees were shocked that this one who claimed to be the Messiah would eat with sinners. They threw that charge in His face all the time.

We should not assume that the invitation arose out of the goodness of Simon's heart. The social customs of the first century would all but require him to entertain important visitors to his town. To snub Jesus would alienate the townsfolk, making a bad situation even worse for Simon.

It is tempting to think, however, that maybe Simon was *intrigued* by Jesus. If you were religious, you could not help but wonder about a person like Jesus. We have all been surprised at how our opinions about people mellow when we have had the opportunity to spend time with them. After hearing Jesus, Simon may have been struck with the sincerity and insight that marked His messages. And of course, he wouldn't have been the first Pharisee to be thus impressed. If Simon wanted to discuss the issues Jesus had raised in his heart, the most natural thing for him to do would be to invite the rabbi to his evening meal. The dinner would provide a forum away from the pushy, noisy crowds to delve into the real issues Jesus had raised. If the evening went as planned, Simon would be able to discern whether Jesus was indeed the prophet He claimed to be.

But to do so was not without risks. Evening meals of the type Simon provided were high-profile events. As we have noted, they were open for noninvitees to come and go as they wished. Eavesdropping on the discussions of important people made for a great night out. Topics would range from politics to civil issues to theology and just about anything else that the invited guests wanted to discuss.

The guests on this evening would have included other influential people from the town. Simon was providing a forum to get to know this intriguing national phenomenon. Jesus would undoubtedly be the center of attention throughout the evening. This kind of setting would cause friends to ask the guests for days afterward, "What was He like? What did He say? What do you think of Him now?" Probably some of Simon's disciples and followers would have been either at the table or among those gathered to listen and watch.

What if Jesus' persuasive powers won the hearts of the influential leaders at the table—to say nothing of the standing-room-only crowd? To show disapproval of Jesus in any way would isolate the Pharisee. The ramifications were many and weighty.

Moreover, inviting Jesus to dinner entailed a risk because the tension between Jesus and the religious establishment was no small secret. The fact that the sinful woman had heard that Jesus would be there indicates how much commotion the invitation had caused among the townspeople.

Whatever the reason and in spite of the risks, Simon had taken a move toward Jesus. In so doing, he was on the brink. He would unwittingly have the potential redeemer of his soul at his table. He didn't know it, but this was the most important dinner party he had ever thrown.

It is here that we may begin to see glimmers of ourselves in Simon's dealings with Jesus.

THE COMFORTABLE DISTANCE

The text doesn't attempt to hide Simon's rudeness. The fact that he doesn't have a servant wash Jesus' feet is a dead giveaway. Footwashing is as common as hanging up a visitor's coat. Nor does Simon greet Jesus with a kiss on the cheek or forehead—the equivalent of a handshake. Surely every other guest has been shown these common courtesies.

The fact that Jesus has not been anointed is less noticeable since one would only anoint a guest who is worthy of special honor—this omission in itself an indication of Simon's attitude toward Jesus.

Why does Simon, having invited Jesus for dinner, treat him so rudely? Clearly, he's playing politics. For all the critics of the invitation— and there are many among Simon's peers—he has made a statement. To those who disapprove, Simon has a defense. He could say that on the one hand it was important to invite this celebrity, but on the other hand he didn't wash His feet or give Him a kiss. And, he could say, "I never anointed Him as an honored guest," which he would have done for every other VIP who had been invited to his table.

So, for all the benefits of having Jesus as a guest, Simon is keeping a comfortable distance. He is careful not to let Jesus' presence threaten his position, power, or standing with friends and colleagues. More importantly, his actions have created a buffer zone in which he can wiggle to maneuver and control the evening and all its ramifications.

Here is where a glance into the mirror might cause us a measure of discomfort. When our identity with Christ and the accompanying commitments begin to threaten our peace, reputation, relationships, or prosperity, it often serves us well to keep Him at a comfortable distance.

I am reminded of Peter's quick distancing of himself from Jesus when the people around the fire accused him of being one of Christ's followers. What was it that intimidated Peter? Damaging his image among those around him? The fear that being implicated with Christ might put his own life in jeopardy? After all, Jesus had just warned His disciples that they would be thrown out of the synagogues and persecuted for His name's sake. So for Peter it was easier to keep his relationship with Christ far from the public view and to outwardly deny Him.

Granted, some of us wouldn't be quite as blatant about setting the distance. Our denials are often far more subtle. Having the opportunity to witness to someone who has power over us or could turn one's back on us or could set tongues wagging may tempt us to set a distance to protect ourselves. Often when I am on a plane, I read my Bible. I tend to wonder what the guy next to me will think. If we are intimidated in a situation like that, we may well set the distance and shield our identity with Christ. In the workplace you may feel that being too open about your faith is far too risky in terms of your colleagues' esteem and your future advancement. Some relationships would evaporate if we let Christ really manage our values and actions. Our dreams and plans would be threatened. Our love for money and all the freedom it gives us most likely will be challenged by an open commitment to Christ. So instead of loving Him more than all of this, we keep Him at a distance to enjoy the short-term rewards of loving life on our own terms.

Instead of loving Him more than all our worldly goods, we keep Him at a distance to enjoy the short-term rewards of loving life on our own terms.

Archbishop Thomas Cranmer lived during the tumultuous time of the Reformation when many in England died as martyrs for their Lord. Just after the coronation of the Roman Catholic queen, Mary Tudor—or "Bloody Mary," as she was called—Cranmer was arrested and spent three years in prison. The queen's emissaries urged him to recant his faith and pledge allegiance to the pope and the doctrines of Rome. He was an old man, then, and the thought of being burned at the stake was more than he could bear, so he signed papers of recantation in order to gain freedom and a peaceful life. At the service where his freedom was supposed to be celebrated, he prayed,

> Oh, Son of God, Redeemer of the World . . .
> Have mercy upon me most . . . miserable sinner,
> I, who have offended more grievously than any can express.
> Whither should I flee for succour? . . . I find no refuge . . .
> Oh, God the Son. . . .
> Although my sins be great, yet Thy Mercy is greater.
> I crave nothing, oh, Lord, for mine own merits,
> but for Thy name's sake, that it may be glorified thereby,
> And for Thy Dear Son Jesus Christ's sake.

Then, to the shock of all who had packed the church on that day, Cranmer said,

> My hand has offended in writing contrary to my heart. Therefore, my hand shall be the first punished, for if I may come to the fire it shall be burned first.[2]

Canceling the recantation of his faith, he was led to the fire, and he died for what he could not deny about Christ. For him, even the flames of a cruel and painful death were not enough to distance his grateful heart from the Christ who had showered his life with such great mercy.

We can understand why Archbishop Cranmer would struggle at the point of life and death. It is much harder to understand why we would struggle with far lesser intimidations.

Think of the hypocrisy of claiming to love Christ while setting a convenient distance in the threatened arenas of our lives. True love is complete love, not merely convenient.

A GUEST WITHOUT HONOR

There is an amazing irony in the fact that Jesus is the only guest at Simon's table who has not been appropriately honored. I want to shout into my Bible, "Simon, you have the almighty Creator of the universe at your table, the King of Kings and Lord of Lords, and you're embarrassed by His presence! Simon, if you only knew who you are entertaining, you would compete with the woman for space at His feet!"

Before we get too critical of Simon, however, let's look again into the mirror. Most of us are delighted to have Christ as a resident guest in our souls, yet if the truth were known, we often give Him less than the honor He is due. He speaks, and we listen only when we want to or are forced to, or when we need Him to bail us out of some jam. He is there for us in case of emergency, accommodated in ways that don't threaten us and dismissed when our needs have been gratified.

A movie shown on television a few years ago, *The End,* illustrates this all-too-prevalent mentality. The main character, Sonny Lawson, discovers that he is dying of an illness and decides to end his life by swimming far out into the ocean. At the last minute he realizes that he really doesn't want to die, so he begins to plead with the Lord to help him make it back to shore. He cries out, "O God! Let me live and I promise to obey every one of the Ten Commandments! I shalt not kill. I shalt not commit adultery. I shalt not . . . I . . . I'll *learn* the Ten Commandments.

Help me make it, Lord, and I'll give you fifty percent of everything I make. Fifty percent, God! I want to point out, God, that *nobody* gives fifty percent! I'm talking gross, God."

Then, as Sonny gets closer to shore and safety, he cries, "I think I'm going to make it! You won't regret this, Lord! I'll obey every commandment. No more cheating in business—once I get rid of those nine acres in the desert. And I'm going to start donating that ten percent right away. I *know* I said fifty percent, Lord. But ten percent to start. If you don't want your ten percent, then don't take it! I know that it was you who saved me. But it was also you who made me sick!"

Don't we know that the God of the universe has set up residence in our hearts? Why, then, do we show Him less courtesy than others to whom we are far less obliged? If we valued who He was and we got a grip on the smallest of things He has done for us, we would strive for ways to honor Him. We would compete for space at His feet—washing, kissing, and anointing Him with sacrificial gifts of our love.

Martie and I are often in social settings where people approach us and engage me in conversation without even a polite acknowledgment of her presence. They rarely look her way, say hello, or extend the common courtesy of a greeting such as, "Hi, I'm Sally. You must be Joe's wife." While I make an effort to introduce and include Martie, the distinct impression one gets in moments like these is that she is there but unimportant. She might as well spend her time humming the Eric Clapton tune "I Must Be Invisible" while the conversation goes on without her. The truth is that if people knew her and how pivotal her influence is in my life, they would find conversation with her far more worth their while. I wonder if Christ ever feels that way about the kind of attention and honor we give Him?

WHERE'S THE PARTY?

One of Simon's faults is that he assumes that the party is at his table. But the real party in his home is taking place at the feet of Jesus. Simon's self-induced blindness causes him to see Jesus as someone who is there to enhance his reputation and help him fulfill his civic and social responsibilities. After all, having the clout to get Jesus to the table is a feather in Simon's power cap: Jesus coming to Simon's table on Simon's terms and for Simon's glory. Simon is the center of his universe, and Jesus is just another person who should orbit around him for the evening.

> *Simon assumes that the party is at his table. But the real party in his home is taking place at the feet of Jesus.*

Do you relate to Christ on the basis of all He can do for you? Is life your party to which Christ has come? Is your relationship with Christ about bringing you peace? Comfort? Purpose? Direction? Eternity? Joy? Well, get up from the table and join the woman at Jesus' feet. Jesus does not exist for us. He does love, help, and provide for us, but the reality is that we exist for Him. Even if He never does anything but sacrifice His life for us, He has done enough to deserve our worship for the rest of our lives. The psalmist recognizes this when he writes,

> Know that the LORD is God.
>> It is he who made us, and we are his;
>> we are his people, the sheep of his pasture.
> Enter his gates with thanksgiving
>> and his courts with praise;
>> give thanks to him and praise His name (Ps. 100:3–4).

Simon is put out because Jesus has not measured up to his expectations. Jesus has sided with the woman who has disrupted and defiled *his* dinner. Indeed, Jesus has ruined Simon's evening. Had Simon believed that the evening was about Jesus and not himself, he would be seeing everything differently. He would realize that Jesus' actions are not just appropriate but profound with meaning. Had he understood, he would join in the forgiven woman's adoration. But it is Simon's party, and Jesus has not followed the script. In the same way, when we don't honor Jesus for being the trustworthy King of our lives, we too will be disappointed with Him.

But Christ *is* the party! We should trust and endorse what He does in our lives by our unflinching allegiance and love. Job knew that life was not about himself but about the God of the universe. Therefore, in the face of confusing disappointment and loss, he was able to say, "Though he slay me, yet will I trust in him" (Job 13:15 KJV).

One of the most difficult things I have had to do as a pastor was to tell a church member that her husband, her son, and her father-in-law had drowned in a fishing accident. This meant that her mother-in-law (who also attended the church) had lost her husband, her son-in-law, and a grandson, and her daughter-in-law (who was about to give birth) had lost her husband, her father-in-law, and her husband's grandfather.

As the days unfolded before and after the funerals, I watched with great admiration the loyalty of these families in the face of such great and unexplainable loss. Broken, confused, and devastated, they kept their eyes fixed on Christ. I can think of only one explanation for that devotion. These families did not expect Christ to offer life on their terms; rather, they trusted Him as the loyal lover of their souls. Regardless.

This past summer I slipped into the back row of a small country church. After a season of praise and worship, the pastor asked a woman to come forward to offer what he called "prayers for the church." She was obviously well prepared. It was a beautifully spoken prayer until she said the words, "And, Lord, we pray this morning for Susan and Peter. . . ." At this point her voice broke, and after failing to get the next couple of words out, she stopped. It was one of those awkward moments when someone publicly begins to cry and can't continue. In a few moments she regained a measure of composure and brokenly prayed, "Lord, we don't know why You have seen fit to take three children from our church family in the last year."

I could hardly believe what I heard—three deaths of children in that small church? I swallowed hard as she continued with a prayer from her heart that I will never forget: "But, Lord, we know that it is not ours to ask why, but to trust You. So, Lord, teach us to trust."

While it is not wrong to ask "why," this woman was right. At the end of every unanswerable question mark is the ultimate question, will we trust Him? Will we cling to the fact that Jesus is the Lord of our lives and that whatever He does will ultimately be worthy of our praise?

Loving Christ is about life at His feet, not about having Him sit with us at our table.

Loving Christ is about life at His feet, not about having Him sit with us at our table. Until we absorb the far-reaching implications of this reality, we will be tempted to *use* Him, not *love* Him.

WHO IS AMONG THE FORGIVEN MUCH?

The toughest glance in the mirror is yet to come. The greatest point of conviction and the most revealing reason why we fail to love Christ more lies in the parable Jesus tells at Simon's party. The occasion for the parable is the obvious tension that has suddenly engulfed the evening. As we have noticed, the dinner is not going well for Simon now that this sinful woman is sobbing at Jesus' feet.

She puts Simon's well-intentioned, demeaning attitude toward Jesus on full display as she pours out the love and honor that Simon has withheld from his deserving guest. In a most dramatic way she silently declares that all that she is and all that she has been—including the tools of her trade—are now His. The perfume that has sweetened her bed and the hair that has been seductively let down are now cleansed as she yields them to Christ. Her life will be new. Nothing she has previously relied on is sufficient. She has clearly found the answer to her soul's search. She has found something far better than the money and attention that men have paid for her services. She is being honest about her sin, and she cannot hold herself back. So she interrupts the party with her adoring expressions of love before the shocked and incredulous dinner guests.

Though disastrously unsettling for Simon, these acts of humble adoration showered on Christ give Simon the moment he is looking for. Any thought that Jesus is who and what He has claimed to be vanish from Simon's mind. Simon now possesses Exhibit A in his self-initiated prosecution of Christ as a fraud. Simon says to himself, "If this man were a prophet, he would know who is touching him and what kind of woman she is—that she is a sinner" (Luke 7:39).

Prophets in Jesus' day were not thought to be clairvoyant but were considered to have special gifts of discernment. No well-schooled religious man would ever allow a sinner such as this to touch him. As we have noted, Simon has gone through strict purification rituals before coming to this meal. Any contact with sin and sinners would be a disqualifying source of defilement. It is difficult to express the disdain and disgust a Pharisee would feel at having this happen at his purified table.

But you've got to love what happens next.

As quickly as the accusation forms in Simon's mind, Jesus bursts the bubble. In a fascinating irony—as if to say, "You don't think I'm a prophet, but I just read your mind"—Jesus turns to His host and says, "Simon, I have something to tell you. . . ." And here He spins the tale that has the sting.

> "Two men owed money to a certain moneylender. One owed him five hundred denarii, and the other fifty. Neither of them had the money to pay him back, so he canceled the debts of both. Now which of them will love him more?"

To which Simon replies,

> "I suppose the one who had the bigger debt canceled."

And Jesus says,

> "You have judged correctly."

Jesus now turns to the woman, but continues to speak to Simon.

"Do you see this woman? I came into your house. You did not give me any water for my feet, but she wet my feet with her tears and wiped them with her hair. You did not give me a kiss, but this woman, from the time I entered, has not stopped kissing my feet. You did not put oil on my head, but she has poured perfume on my feet" (Luke 7:40–46).

Jesus then makes the most profound yet clearest point about loving Him: Those who are forgiven much love much. Read no further. Put the book down and consider the depth and breadth of this life-transforming statement: *Loving Christ is a response from a heart that is taken captive by the awareness of how much we have been forgiven . . . a response from a heart that gladly admits a debt of gratitude that a lifetime of good works can only begin to repay.*

The Brooklyn Tabernacle Choir was singing in Chicago several years ago, and I was as taken with the singers as much as I was with their songs. The sincerity and depth of feeling they brought to the music showed that this was more than a mere performance. As they interspersed the music with testimonies, I realized how many in the choir had been redeemed from the pit of sin in Brooklyn.

> *Loving Christ is a response from a heart that is taken captive by the awareness of how much we have been forgiven.*

One song in particular captured my attention: "I'm Not Afraid Anymore." The powerful lyrics penetrated my heart. For us who live in safe environments, it is hard to identify with the lyrics, but they were being sung on that Saturday afternoon by people who used to live in constant fear: fear of violence, fear of not having enough money, fear of what might happen to their children, fear of not being able to get the drugs needed to feed their addictions, fear of every tomorrow. As the soloist sang the powerful words, the spotlights showed tears trickling down his cheeks. Later I learned why he wept as he sang.

His name is Calvin Hunt. Although he was married and had several children, his family life had been less than ideal. He recalls,

> I got really messed up with crack cocaine, and I hit bottom because of it. I would be out on the streets for days, even weeks, without ever coming home or calling. I would go places and do things I never would have in my right frame of mind. There were people armed with weapons, people giving up their children sexually to men for drugs in these crack dens. It was like a glimpse of hell. When the money ran out, I would come back home pitiful and sorry and really out of it. My wife was always there, and she would always accept me back home. Then I would work and do the same thing all over the next payday. This went on for four years.
>
> One day my daughter brought home a flyer for a movie entitled *Cry For Freedom,* about young people hooked on crack, and it was my life story. That night I gave my heart to the Lord and I started attending church, but I kept falling and coming back. The pastors were trying to get me into a program, but I resisted. I felt I could stop by myself, but that didn't work. I ran from their help for a year, until the pastor finally told me he had nothing else to tell me, that he had done all that he could in the Lord. I felt alone, like nowhere to run, and I finally surrendered and went into the program. I had to give up and surrender everything for the Lord to work in me.
>
> That was several years ago. and I thank God for finding me and picking me up from that.[3]

Today Calvin sings of not being afraid anymore and stirs thousands each year singing songs such as "Mercy Saw Me" and "I'm Clean."

And every time he sings you get the distinct impression that these songs come from the heart of one who has been forgiven much.

When was the last time you viewed yourself as someone forgiven much? Far too often we assign that privilege to those who have been dredged up by the grace of God from the sludge of life. Those who are forgiven much are the prostitutes, rapists, drug addicts, spouse abusers, and child molesters who have been discovered by grace. We do not readily see ourselves as being numbered among the Calvin Hunts of our world, the Ruth McBrides, the thief on the cross, Paul the persecutor of the church, or even the woman at Jesus' feet. These kind of folk are at best a curious lot whom we find interesting and even admirable, but we do not count ourselves among them.

The problem is that most of us feel we live pretty good lives by comparison. Yet the most telling point in Jesus' conversation with Simon is what He tacks on to the end of the "forgiven much" statement.

When Jesus tells Simon that he who is forgiven little loves little, we might, if we are not careful, assume that He is saying, "Look, Simon, you're a pretty good guy. You don't live on the seamy side of life. You are not in the grip of addictions to sin like others. In fact, Simon, you have a reputation for keeping all the laws and codes to the very letter. You and I really are more like colleagues in this enterprise of righteousness. I'm really quite proud of you, Simon, and since there is not much in your life to forgive you for, I really don't expect you to love me all that much."

There is not a chance in all of eternity that this is what Jesus means. In Jesus' eyes, the Pharisees take pride in their own righteousness and are deeply offensive to God. Their sins are the hidden sins of the heart. Resting on the laurels of external conformity, they are blind to the inner defilement of pride, hypocrisy, and lack of compassion for sinners. The Pharisees' inner lust for power will ultimately show itself as they lie about Jesus in order to have Him put to death in a murderous conspiracy.

Jesus is never at a loss for words to point out the deep sin and the damaged heart condition of these religious leaders. He has zero tolerance for their self-flaunting behavior and the oppressive religious drills they force on others in the name of God, drills that provide a platform on which they can publicly strut the stuff of their well-practiced lives. Any thought that Jesus is impressed by their self-serving brand of righteousness vanishes when He calls them "whited sepulchres" (Matt. 23:27 KJV), that is, "whitewashed tombs."

What, then, is Jesus saying to Simon . . . and to us?

In essence He says, "Simon, your problem is that you don't *think* you need to be forgiven much. And because you don't feel you need to be forgiven much, you do not love me much."

> *"You don't love me much because you don't believe you have been forgiven much."*

It is here that my resemblance to Simon bothers me most.

I accepted Christ as Savior when I was six. I grew up in a Christian home and have served Him in ministry most of my life. It is hard to see myself among the "forgiven much," which makes me a lot like Simon.

The loving gratitude that results in a transformed life can only come when we grasp both the depth of our sin and the depth of God's grace in Jesus Christ. Let's face it: getting a love-stirring grip on God's grace is a challenge. The most lethal stroke of the adversary is to make us lose sight of the saving work of Jesus and to take His extensive grace for granted. When we succumb to this, we are rendered little more than religious robots, mechanically bound to programmed actions and responses. God wants a grace-born affection that drives us to spontaneous and sometimes risky, even radical expressions of love.

And, I might add, we grow accustomed to His grace because we so easily develop a distorted view of ourselves. Without a continuing awareness of why grace is so necessary, we are lulled into forming an exaggerated perspective of our own worth before God. After all, none of us are as bad as the next guy and certainly not as bad as the rapist or the serial killer. We who have lived in the church culture for a long time have put our lives into fairly decent shape. We keep most of the rules, say the right things, serve, sit, soak, and feel quite satisfied. The longer we are in the kingdom of God, the better we feel about ourselves. After all, we are pretty good people . . . His kind of people—the kind who really don't need to be forgiven much.

So what Jesus says to Simon can also be said of us: "You don't love me much because you don't believe you have been forgiven much." For all who want to love Christ more than with the mind or will, that is a stinging reproof. It is a reproof that should cause us to ask for a renewed and realistic view of ourselves and the love-inducing grace that flows from God.

CHAPTER FIVE

THE PHARISEE IN ALL OF US

The Eclipse of Devotion

Early in our marriage I had to learn Martie's love language. As you may know, people have different ways in which they feel loved. If you were loved by touch as you grew up, then touching is a way you feel loved. For others, feeling loved may come through affirming words, through gifts, or through acts of kindness. It is a relational disaster when two lovers miss the love language of each other.

I came into our marriage with the assumption that flowers were the universal language of love. If we believe the FTD commercials, every woman wilts at the mention of a fragrant bouquet. So one evening I did the old dozen-roses-behind-my-back, kiss-on-the-cheek routine, fully believing Martie would swoon in my arms. She graciously thanked me, sniffed them, smiled, and took them to the kitchen to put them in water.

I must admit, it was not exactly the response I had expected. Less than impressed, I followed her into the kitchen and asked if perhaps she didn't like the flowers. She said that she liked them a lot, but wondered how much money they had cost. I was a seminary student at the time, and money was tight. As I recall, the flowers cost more than the monthly rent at the seminary's housing. So it's understandable that to Martie the flowers were an unnecessary expense in an already endangered budget. To me, they were a message of love.

The flowers didn't connect. My assumptions and Martie's expectations were miles apart. Actually, after all these years I have learned that her love language is about far more expensive things than flowers. I'm not thinking about "stuff"—it's my time and attention that makes her feel loved. I'd like to have a five-dollar bill for every time she has said, "Have you heard anything I have said?" Worse yet, she can be expounding on a great theme for minutes on end and then close the discourse by saying, "What do you think?" I'm embarrassingly stuck. My only resort is to ask in return, "Well, what do you think about it?" in the hope that I can pick up a clue from which to form a relatively intelligent response and dodge the bullet. Paying attention to Martie convinces her that she has value and worth and that her thoughts and perspectives are important to me. Joining her and affirming her in her world say "I love you" in far deeper tones than flowers.

It is clear from Scripture that well-intentioned people can think they love Christ yet totally miss the mark.

It should come as no surprise that Jesus has a love language. The Bible is full of descriptions, exhortations, and illustrations of the kind of love that *touches* the heart of Christ. It is also clear from Scripture that well-intentioned people can think they love Him yet totally miss the mark. An ironic point of the story of Simon and the sinful woman is that Jesus affirms the love of a maligned sinner and reproves the lovelessness of the good guy in town.

LIVING LIFE LOVELESSLY

It is a sobering thought to realize that in all of our goodness, our busyness for Christ, and our behavioral conformity, we may not be connecting with Him at all. Simon the Pharisee would have proudly proclaimed that He loved God. He more than anyone else had groomed his life to conform to the codes and traditions of the law. He had mastered even the smallest nuances of religious requirements. For him to cringe from the intrusive display of affection by the sinful woman was an instinctively religious response. Yet Jesus endorsed her love as authentic and Simon's as a failing love. Simon thought he was good; Jesus had a surprisingly different view.

Simon brings to mind my all-time favorite nursery rhyme, "Little Jack Horner." Little Jack is sitting in a corner indulging himself with a Christmas pie. He sticks in his thumb and pulls out a plum and says, "What a good boy am I." The story makes Jack look like a poster boy for goodness. After all, in his mind he was good, and through all of the years of the telling of the story, no one has disputed the claim. But a closer look at Jack gives cause for concern. What is he doing sitting in a corner?

My recollection has it that only bad boys end up sitting in corners. Most of the pictures of little Jack have him holding a whole pie on his lap. I have never known a mother to give a child a whole pie. Perhaps he has stolen this from the kitchen, to say nothing of the fact that he is taking credit for something he didn't do. He could at least have given the credit to his mother for putting the plums there. Anyway, what did he expect to find in a plum pie? And, if you don't like my analysis to this point, then I have to ask you, what is he doing with his fingers in the food? He has violated the most fundamental principles of table manners. Yet he proudly considers himself worthy of praise for his self-proclaimed goodness.

Simon is not much better. Blinded by his perception of himself and the praise of others, he is totally unaware that his life does not please or communicate love to the God he so jealously serves. We have to keep in mind that it is not what we think about ourselves that counts. It is what Christ thinks of us.

Like most of us, I have to be constantly on guard to focus my life on loving Christ. For reasons best known to our Lord, He has put me in a high-profile ministry. People assume that you are a good person when you serve in leadership. When there are a lot of "attaboys," it is easy to measure spiritual success by the applause.

Anyone who assumes that Christianity is about garnering applause for good behavior has only to read Revelation 2. It shatters the notion that busyness and behavioral conformity are the same as loving Christ. The church at Ephesus was doing all the right things. In fact, if you didn't know the rest of the story, you might nominate them for church of the year. Yet Christ had a different view. He said that He had something against them. To hear Christ size up our lives like that is a scary thought. Christ called the church to repent and warned that if they did not, He would remove their power and effectiveness.

The charge against them? They had, as He said, left their "first love." By that He did not mean the way they felt when they first came to Christ. He was reproving them because their love for Christ was not the moving priority of their lives. Their good deeds were not done out of a love for Christ, but for lesser reasons. Simply put, they did what they did for all the wrong reasons. Perhaps their good behavior was spurred by a sense of religious obligation. Or they may have tried to live up to the expectations of others. Their obedience may have been driven by the fear of consequences. They may have given because they thought they would be blessed in return. Or perhaps their good works and tenacious defense of the faith were for some kind of self-centered interest— the applause of others, pride, position, or power.

Whatever the motivation, one thing is certain: It wasn't done out of a love for Christ. Their good works were not about Him, for Him, or because of Him. Hence, Christ's reproof. In His eyes, their "good works" were ultimately good for nothing.

THE TROUBLE WITH A DUTIFUL LIFE

We should all be warned that there is a well-traveled detour on our way to heaven. It leads down the dead-end street of becoming consumed with the agenda of our goodness and causes us to lose touch with the one who made the agenda possible in the first place. When that happens, everything goes sour. The only way to avoid this disaster is to cultivate a Christianity that is singly and simply about loving Christ.

Oswald Chambers writes,

> We consider what we do in the way of Christian work as service, yet Jesus Christ calls service to be what we are to Him, not what we do for Him. Discipleship is based solely on devotion to Jesus Christ. . . . Today we have substituted doctrinal belief for personal belief, and that is why so many people are devoted to causes and so few are devoted to Jesus Christ.[1]

Christianity is not first and foremost about our *doing;* it is about what He has *done.* It is not about what we are becoming; it is about what He has become for us. As a result, all we do and all we are becoming are a response to His loving acts of grace and mercy. Whenever we lose touch with that motivation, we cease to speak His love language.

Christianity is not first and foremost about our doing; *it is about what He has* done.

Martie would get no satisfaction if she thought I helped with the housework, stayed faithful to her, took her out to dinner, remembered our anniversary, and frequently said, "I love you," simply because these are the kinds of things a good husband does. She would be even more offended if I did them merely because I was committed to the institution of marriage. Doing things for Martie is always the best when I love her. The best love is not about me. The best love is about her, because of her, and for her. When it is about me and what I do, then the villain pride soon consumes my soul.

But it is not just pride that snares us. When our Christianity is primarily about duty and doing, we eventually become tired of being good for goodness' sake. When Christianity is not practiced out of loving gratitude for Christ, it soon becomes dull, boring, and burdensome. We quickly become judgmental. A materially exotic and sensually erotic environment stands ready to seduce and destroy hearts that have grown weary in well doing. And if by sheer resolve we hang in there and keep at it, our fate is to become more like Simon every day.

As one observer keenly notes, this kind of pharisaical approach to Christianity leaves one

> humorless, prudish, constrained in his affections, incapable of enjoying himself, repressed, inhibited, pouting and censorious.
>
> There are hundreds of people like that today: respectable, conventional, good people. They look down their noses at the permissive society; they curl their lip at the decay in moral standards. They think they're good, but they are not; they're simply dull. They think they're being moral, but they are not; they're simply feeling sanctimonious.
>
> Joyless in their hypocrisy, sterile in their respectability, their religion has no more in common with Christianity than a frigid marriage has in common with a real love affair.[2]

I remember asking a student at Moody Bible Institute about her boyfriend. She said nothing about what he does for her or about the gifts he gives. She simply said, "He adores me!" We have to ask if that is how Christ feels about our love for Him.

When Christianity is not practiced out of loving gratitude for Christ, it soon becomes dull, boring, and burdensome, and we become judgmental.

As Michelangelo wrote about his transformation from living to do good to doing good to express his love for Christ, "My soul turned to that love divine that spread its arms on the cross to take us in." Our souls must turn there as well.

Christianity is always about the One who has loved us and given Himself for us. But when we drift from this motivation and begin to be good because we are Christians, then our goodness quickly elevates self instead of the Savior. When this happens, the door is wide open for arrogance to creep into our well-intentioned heart. Eclipsing the preeminent place of the Son is a serious and damaging distortion.

Weird things happen when the moon eclipses the sun. The moon, which is intended to be the lesser light that reflects the power and warmth of the sun, becomes the center of attention. The warmth of the sun is chilled by the eclipsing presence of the moon. The sky turns a dullish gray, and there is an eerie sense that something is not right. It may be a great moment for the moon, but it's not a great moment for anything else, particularly the sun.

This was Simon's problem. This is our problem. This is about the Pharisee that lives in all of us.

THE PHARISEE IN ALL OF US

Since the Pharisees are often the bad guys of the Gospels, it is easy to feel that we are not afflicted with their problems. After all, we are close to Christ. If Christ were here today, we would be His followers. But before we get too smug, we must remind ourselves that the Pharisees did not start out to be bad guys. They really wanted to be good for God. Their drift from authenticity to self-absorbed religiosity was subtle and extremely deceptive. No well-intentioned reader of this book is exempt from the same fate. And as strange as it may seem, the slippery slope is greased by desiring and succeeding at being good.

The Pharisees did not start out to be bad guys.
Their drift from authenticity to self-absorbed
religiosity was subtle and extremely deceptive.

There are at least four dynamics that threaten any well-behaved relationship with Christ. Use them as a measure for your heart.

1. *The better we become, the more impressed we are with ourselves.* Jesus noted that the Pharisees enjoyed praying in public and went to great lengths to ensure that people knew they were fasting. They threw their money noisily into the large trumpet-shaped depositories at the temple door to be sure that others knew of their gifts.

That is really the weird thing about being good. When we do good things, we like the attention, and then we are no longer very good even while we continue to do good things. After a series of sermons about servanthood, I took the responsibility to pour everyone's coffee at the next meeting of the church board. As I was "serving," one of the deacons remarked, "Look, our pastor has a servant's heart!" I loved the sound of it. I poured coffee again at the next meeting, but now for a different reason. In the darkest corners of my heart I was hoping people would again notice that I was being a servant, which really meant I was serving to serve myself.

A parent of a student at Moody recently wrote and said how much their daughter was getting out of her experience, and that she appreciated me and thought I was a very humble man. As I read the letter, that particular part had a good ring to it. In fact, if I am not careful I might just enjoy writing about it in this book.

It is hard to love God when we love ourselves more. Actually, it is impossible. Therein lies the irony: We start out to love God and end up loving ourselves.

2. *The better we become, the greater distance we set between ourselves and those who are not as good.* The infamous prayer of the Pharisees, "Lord, I thank you that I am not like . . . ," reflects the proud distance their goodness had created. It never occurred to them that we are all really just beggars telling other beggars where to find bread. Regardless of how we try to cover ourselves on this matter, most of us feel that we really are better than those who "live in sin." But we are not better—not at all. We are forgiven, Spirit-enabled, and directed people who are

good only because Someone Else came along and made it possible. We may behave better, but we are not better. When our behavior blinds us to this fundamental reality about ourselves, we become sanctimonious, judgmental, uncompassionate, and disinterested in the spiritual welfare of those whose only hope is Christ.

Lisa DePalma is a recent Moody graduate who has a very effective ministry among the prostitutes on Chicago's west and north sides. On Friday and Saturday nights she walks the streets with a ministry companion to engage street girls with the liberating good news of Jesus Christ. Always chaperoned by two men who walk a half block behind, she reaches out to these enslaved women. They hear that they no longer need to live under the bondage of drugs and the cruel mastery of their pimps. Always used and never loved, they hear—some of them for the first time—that God has wonderfully loved them in Jesus Christ.

Recently I sat in a small gathering as Lisa talked about the women she encounters. The women in our group were stunned at the thought of bartering one's body for drug money. I wondered if it crossed any of their minds that they could be among those prostitutes if it hadn't been for the tremendous advantages of God's grace in their lives. For that matter, I could have been the pimp that ran the business.

Are there degrees of fallenness? Are there any privileged births when it comes to having a sinful nature? Am I not just as fallen as they? Without the home I grew up in, the experience of redemption, the supernatural edge of the indwelling Spirit, and a dozen other privileges of grace, I could be there. We all could. Our understanding of this truth must penetrate us more deeply than the worn cliché, "There but for the grace of God go I!" The reality should make our very souls shudder at the thought of where we might be today if it hadn't been for Him. The thought ought to drive us to love Him passionately for the undeserved rescue He launched on our behalf. It should cure us once and for all of the sanctimonious aloofness that often plagues our kind of Christianity.

Lisa wrote a poem that expresses a loving heart's perspective.

Can you see her? Will you let God show you?
Her face instead of her clothes?
Her eyes instead of her body?
Can you see her? Will you let God show you?
She has a name instead of a label
A broken heart instead of a hard one
Can you see her? Will you let God show you?
The image of God instead of an object of scorn
Her worth to the Savior instead of her worthlessness to the world
Can you see her? Will you let God show you?
His heart of forgiveness instead of your heart that judges
His blood that covers instead of your rules that condemn
Can you see her? Will you let God show you?
And when you do see, what then?

I wish Lisa had been there to whisper these words to Simon as he watched with revulsion the outpouring of the prostitute's love at Jesus' feet. His well-conformed life had shut her out. Jesus was welcoming her in.

3. *The better we feel we are becoming, the more godless we may be.* The Pharisees became so fond of being good that they kept inventing new traditions and codes to obey. They may have felt, as some of us do, that "strictness is next to godliness." But in the process they became more strict than God. In fact, Jesus reproved them for placing spiritual burdens on people that God never intended. Godliness means to be like God. Any addition to or subtraction from who He is, what He is like, and what He requires is a move away from godliness. Ungodliness is not always about the really bad people. It is about the really good people who are more restrictive than God.

Godliness means to be like God. Any addition to or subtraction from who He is, what He is like, and what He requires is a move away from godliness.

The Pharisees' good intentions led them astray. They took the laws of God and added extra rules for good measure. These were called "fence laws." Since women were the source of temptation and moral failure, the Pharisees decided that a rabbi was not to touch, talk to, or walk on the same side of the street as a woman. This helped them avoid any chance of breaking the law against adultery. While these may have been helpful as guidelines, the fence laws were given the weight of divine law. They had fence laws about the Sabbath, about purity, and just about anything that had to do with righteous living. This is exactly the reason that Jesus was so unpopular with them. He jealously kept His Father's law but ignored their fence laws.

Those who lived through the sixties recall that the hippie subculture in the United States represented the antithesis of just about everything that believers held sacred. Hippies advocated free love and communal living. Drugs released them from the constraints of authority. Rebellion against all that was proper and "straight" was the theme of the day.

The hippies had a certain style, and we could easily spot them in a crowd. The men wore their hair long and often sported unkempt beards. Their instrument of choice was the guitar. To avoid being confused with a godless subculture, Christians were quick to "avoid the appearance of evil." Boys were not allowed to have hair that extended over their ears, and faces were always shaven.

Hair length and beardlessness soon became marks of spirituality. Churches adopted the standards for choir and platform personnel. Colleges added the rules to their student handbooks. I have no argument with establishing appropriate boundaries. The problem is that soon these standards carried equal weight with revealed laws of righteousness. Then, when the hippie movement faded off the scene, we forgot to drop the rules.

Well into the eighties, long after the subculture had disappeared, many churches and organizations still enforced these rules. Male students at Moody had to keep their hair off their ears and could not wear beards (which is ironic, since D. L. Moody had a beard, and his pictures are everywhere on campus). One of the downsides of rules is trying to defend them when their relevance has passed. Assigning the weight of God's will to our preferences inevitably alienates thoughtful people and makes God look unduly restrictive and irrelevant, which is a rap that He doesn't deserve.

Principles of righteousness never change; however, the applications of righteous principles must remain fluid. The well-meaning Pharisees encumbered God's people with their extrapolated goodness and became unlike Him.

4. *The better we become, the more we feel God is impressed.* Jesus was not impressed with the Pharisees' proud, hypocritical brand of righteousness. The better they had become on the outside, the worse they had become on the inside. This is why Jesus called them "whitewashed tombs" (Matt. 23:27). If you were a Pharisee, this was a stinging indictment. Graves were sources of defilement. At feast times the Pharisees would actually whitewash the grave sites so they would clearly stand out on the landscape. That way every one could see them and avoid becoming ceremonially defiled.

Jesus' word picture was meant to reveal the Pharisees as clean on the outside but defiled as death on the inside. We must always remember that man looks on the outward appearance, but God looks at our hearts. He is not impressed with what we do if it masks who we really are on the inside.

For Simon, this was the problem. His externally spit-polished life had blinded him to his true condition.

I have always been intrigued by the prophet Nathan's approach when he was confronting King David with charges of adultery and murder (2 Sam. 12). Nathan was in a precarious position. Accusing the king of such tawdry actions meant the prophet's risking his life. Wisely, Nathan crafted a story of a wealthy man who had many sheep but took a lamb from the flock of his impoverished neighbor. When Nathan asked David how he felt about someone who would do such a thing,

David was infuriated and spoke in the harshest terms about what the wicked rich man deserved. Then, in a dramatic moment of truth, Nathan said, "You are the man!"

In a very real sense, Simon's response to Jesus and the woman may be Nathan's finger in our face. When we are honest with ourselves, we see an awful lot of Simon in our hearts.

YOU TOO COULD BE A PHARISEE

One wonders how Simon could get so far off course in the pursuit of goodness. The Pharisees were so stuck in the routines of self-righteousness that they didn't even recognize God when He arrived. Nor did Simon recognize true worship and adoration when he saw it. He was so impressed with his own goodness that he couldn't see true goodness when it dined with him at his table, and when it abruptly interrupted his routine.

The Pharisees were so stuck in the routines of self-righteousness that they didn't even recognize God when He arrived.

I often wonder what I would do if Christ were to threaten the norms and traditions of my sense of true religion. It is important to ask ourselves whether we would be free to embrace Him or, like the Pharisees, would resist. It would be frightening to be deeply religious yet deeply wrong.

A look at the spiritual mindset of the Pharisees may help us see why we tend to be modern-day Simons. Granted, many of the "good people" of Christ's day were godly, pious individuals honestly seeking God and the truth. Certainly Nicodemus's visit to Jesus reflects that some Pharisees were both intrigued and interested in His claims. But the fact that Nicodemus came by night demonstrates that relationships between Jesus and the religious leaders of His day were already strained.

None of the Pharisees woke up in the morning and said, "I know I am wrong, but I am going to oppose Jesus." They really believed they were right, and their view of Jesus as a radical revolutionary who was deceiving the people was a sincere outgrowth of all they believed.

The Pharisees were a society of pious men who were zealous for keeping the law. Their very name is from the Aramaic root word that means "separate," designating them as being distinct from the general public. This distinctiveness was marked in their disciplined adherence to the law. They were not only the law's keepers and exemplary advocates but also the interpreters of its regulations. They were the "good works" police.

This helps us understand their total disdain for people they called "sinners." Sinners were second only to tax collectors in the hierarchy of the Pharisees' "worst-kind-of-people" list. Sinners were those who lived outside the restraints of the law—or the law as manufactured by the Pharisees—and who refused to pay attention to the details of the law.

That is the reason for the Pharisees' suspicion and discomfort with Jesus. Their legalistic expression of faith crossed swords with Jesus in many ways. Jesus came as the perfect revelation of God's will and ways. He could not endorse their burdensome, man-made system and still give a true picture of the freedom of God's brand of right living. So He lived outside their rules yet within the boundaries of His Father.

His teachings also reproved them. Jesus challenged the validity of their traditions. He championed humility in the face of their pride. He taught the value of servanthood in contrast to their love of power and control. Jesus counted the heart important, not merely the external trappings of a highly disciplined life. He had zero tolerance for the Pharisees' duplicity and hypocrisy, but deep compassion for even the worst of sinners. Jesus spoke of a righteousness that was a gift from God and resisted those who sported their own brand of self-made righteousness.

But more importantly, Jesus and the Pharisees were miles apart on the nature of His mission. Jesus came to prove that God is interested in sinners. Even tax collectors. That shocked the sensitivities of the

Pharisees to the core. In fact, they tried to discredit Him by announcing to anyone who would hear, "This man spends time with sinners and eats with them."

In an effort to explain His choice of dinner companions, Jesus tells three stories: the stories of the lost lamb, the lost coin, and the lost son (Luke 15). All of these are intended to communicate that sinners have worth and value to God and that He is interested in seeking and saving them if they will respond. To a crowd that envisions grace as God's reward for the good guys, and judgment as the only fitting response to sinners, this does not compute—especially coming from one who claims to be the Son of God.

A. M. Hunter observes that "the new thing in Christianity is not the doctrine that God saves sinners. No Jew would have denied that. It is the assertion that God loves them and saves them as sinners."[3]

It is against this backdrop of religiosity that we watch Simon interact with Jesus and this sinful woman.

We may feel that none of us live at such odds with Christ as did the religious rulers of His day. But let's not excuse ourselves too quickly. As we have tried to make clear, it is easy to feel quite good about ourselves because we have faithfully conformed to what we believe to be God's ways, especially compared with others who have no time for the righteous ways of God. Are the "worst of sinners" in our world loved and sought by us, or are we more likely to condemn and ostracize them in an effort to keep our lives and culture "clean"? Do we in our goodness feel twinges of pride, and are we ever tempted to think that our goodness is something that we have developed because we are well-disciplined good people? Has our goodness become a habit, or does it thrive as a response? When was the last time you assumed that external conformity to goodness was sufficient for pleasing God? Do you ever feel a twinge of jealousy when others are more revered than you? Is there any sense of hypocrisy or duplicity in your life? Are you genuinely touched when you sing the words that He "saved a wretch like me," or does that refer to someone else? When was the last time you reproved the pride that lurks in the shadows of your heart?

---

*If we are honest with ourselves, we all struggle with
the little Pharisee within who wants to grow up
and dominate our spirituality.*

Any "guilty as charged" response to these questions should alert us to the possibility that we have left our first love and have been co-opted by the system instead of being overwhelmed by the Savior.

If we are honest with ourselves, we all struggle with the little Pharisee within who wants to grow up and dominate our spirituality. When we let this happen, we abort the life-transforming capacity to embrace Christ as the reason for who we are and what we do. After all, it is difficult to celebrate Christ's amazing goodness in our lives if we are celebrating our own. When we are impressed with our own goodness, our love for Christ will diminish. Then we will qualify for the dubious honor of loving little and find ourselves loving little and sitting with Simon far from the Master's feet.

CHAPTER SIX

BARRIERS TO LOVE

Confusing My Goodness with His Greatness

I had never thought much about Stradivarius violins except for the well-worn joke that fathers-of-the-bride-to-be tell: "I feel like I'm handing over a Stradivarius to a two-hundred-pound gorilla." Then I met Erin, my nephew's friend. Erin is an accomplished violinist who is studying at one of the nation's most prestigious music conservatories. While I love the beauty of a well played violin, I must admit that my worst music memories are from the violin sections in the elementary school music programs Martie and I attended to support our children. So I asked Erin what it takes to play a violin well.

Erin said that beautiful violin music is about the way you hold the instrument, the way you hold the bow, the way you touch the strings with the bow, the way you hold your arm, and the quality of the instrument. Her instructor had recently told her that in order to go to the next level of achievement, she would need a better violin—which would cost more than $30,000. A new bow to go with it would cost between $10,000 and $15,000. Immediately my mind turned to the value of a Stradivarius. I asked Erin if she had ever heard one played. She had, and she noted that you can easily tell the difference between a Stradivarius and another violin. Her dream was to place a Stradivarius under her chin and experience its beauty personally.

Stradivarius had a touch that no other violinmaker has ever been able to duplicate. Today, nearly three hundred years after his death, his violins remain without peer in tone, quality, and playability. The few that exist are worth hundreds of thousands of dollars. Many of them are lodged in well-secured display cases in great museums, to be removed only on the rare occasion when they are lent for a special event to a select few virtuosos who demonstrate their rare worth in concert.

I would imagine that if violins had life, they would all want to have been touched by the hand of the master violin maker. The few that were would no doubt speak of the joy and beauty of their lives, all of which they owed to Stradivarius. But they would also relate how they had their beginnings in the sludge of the polluted harbor in the village of Cremona, Italy, where Antonius Stradivarius had his shop.

THE PIT FROM WHICH WE HAVE BEEN DUG

Loving Christ is most often sabotaged by not knowing or, worse yet, forgetting where we have come from and where we would be today if we had not been transformed by the hand of the Master.

When we trivialize our true condition and downplay our need of God's matchless grace it becomes impossible to express a love born of gratitude. In the process we become much like Simon. The thought that in some way I am akin to the self-righteous object of Jesus' censure brings back the same feelings I had when I would get caught hanging around with the wrong crowd at school. In the story in Luke 7, Simon *is* the wrong crowd—big time.

Living in Chicago makes me well aware of Christ's power to dramatically change a life. Many of my friends are street warriors who take the liberating message of Christ to the most despairing of sinners. On occasion I hear the testimonies of those who have been snatched by Jesus out of the jaws of defeat and despair.

Arloa Sutter founded Breakthrough Ministries, which takes the love of Christ to the homeless on the streets of Chicago. Many of these people have been destroyed by poor choices or have been victimized since birth. They are living examples of the life-destroying power of sin. At a banquet celebrating the work of Arloa's ministry, a man was asked to give his testimony. He told of the deep change that Christ had brought to his life. Arloa glowed with joy as she related that this man had lived for years as a homeless vagrant, but now holds down a full-time job, has his own apartment, and witnesses the life-changing grace of Jesus every day. In addition, he volunteers in her ministry, reaching out to others who are still in the bondage from which he has been freed. But when I heard the rest of the man's story, I wanted to cry for the wonderful love of Christ to pursue even the worst of us.

Arloa was speaking at the Moody's Founders Week conference a couple of years ago. Since the conference is broadcast nationally, the next day she received a call from a couple in Ohio. Hearing her on the radio, they wondered if Arloa could help them find their son, who was living as a homeless man in Chicago. They were heart-broken and had given up all hope until they heard Arloa that night. Aware that there are thousands of homeless in the city, she told them that it would be nearly impossible to find him. Not wanting to take no for an answer they told her that they thought he usually spent most of his time near the forest preserve and was often seen hanging around the liquor store there. Much to everyone's surprise, the store owner found him, put him in the car, and brought him to Breakthrough, where two days later he accepted the Lord. Rehabilitated he now lives to help others find the Christ who liberated his soul.

The next year we had Arloa bring Jim to Founders Week where he gave a stirring testimony about the impact of Christ's saving grace. He literally glowed with enthusiasm for Jesus. As he put it, "Once this freight train got out of the station it's been a cannonball express and it ain't stopped yet!"

*To think that we haven't been saved from much
leaves us feeling that we don't have the need to be
forgiven much.*

Such stories of redemption from alcohol, crack abuse, prostitu-
tion, and crime often leave me feeling somewhat cheated. It is not that
I would want the struggles and the baggage resulting from these sins,
but rather that these, once redeemed, seem to love Christ in a special
way. They weep with joy at what He has done for them. Their lives are
driven by heartfelt love and they live to thank Christ for what He has
done. They have the edge on those of us who have far less dramatic rescue stories to tell. Yet, isn't that very thought our problem? To think that
we haven't been saved from much leaves us feeling that we really haven't
been forgiven much. And, as Jesus noted, that may be the reason that
we don't truly love Him as much.

Loving Him demands getting a realistic view of our desperately
fallen condition and embracing a fresh glimpse of the extensive mercy
and grace of God. Making this shift is not easy.

Our lives are busy and distracted. We live to think the best of ourselves. We spend our money to enhance our image, or at least to achieve
a level of decent social acceptance. Our cars, houses, wardrobes, friends,
and bank accounts all testify to our all-rightness. So, to see ourselves as
abjectly bankrupt sinners before a pure and just God requires a revolutionary reality check. But loving Christ goes nowhere until we make
the shift.

I was in our employee coffee shop when a colleague casually
greeted me with the familiar, "How are you today?"

To which I replied, "Better than I deserve."

"Oh no, you deserve a lot" was his gracious reply. But to be honest, I had to respond, "Actually I deserve hell, so everything today beyond
that is a bonus."

He seemed taken back by that . . . he shouldn't have been.

You may be thinking, "I don't like to trash myself and go through life thinking that I am nothing." That's just the point. Sin has already taken care of that. We've been trashed by sin's debilitating bondage since birth. But wonderfully, Jesus has taken care of the problem (Col. 1:12–13). By His unbelievable mercy, through no merit of our own, He has recycled us to become new and worthy in Him (Gal 2:20). It is for grace like this that we live to love Him.

In my own pilgrimage toward loving Christ more deeply and consistently, I have struggled with three specific obstacles to a realistic view of my plight before God. These same obstacles would have been Simon's as well.

Parentage

As a boy Simon no doubt went to the Sabbath school, where he would have been trained by the local rabbis and Pharisees. Early in life he would have been formed and framed by the laws of the Old Testament; the codes and traditions of his fathers would have governed his entire perspective on life. Simon was a "lifer" and had obviously been good for most of his earthly existence. It is hard to appreciate redemption when it feels as if it has always been there.

As I have mentioned, I accepted Christ at the age of six. So the bad things I was redeemed from consisted of biting my sister and not picking up my room. Being a third-generation follower, I could do the church thing blindfolded with my hands tied behind my back regardless of Christ. My guess is that the theology student who asked me, "What does it really mean to love Christ?" was, like me, a lifer with Jesus. Otherwise, he may not have asked the question.

For those of us who have grown up as Christians, there can be a sense that Christ really has not done much for us at all. We forget that if He never does anything more than rescue us from eternity in hell and thereby guarantee heaven, He has already done far more than we deserve, enough to fill us with adoring love for Him all the way home.

But Christ has done much for us. Do you ever contemplate where you might be today if He had not rescued you early on?

Even though I was a kid when I asked Christ to save me, as an adult I have a growing sense of love-inducing gratitude. I tremble to think of what might have been if I had not been touched by His grace. I wonder what my self-centeredness might have done to treasured relationships with Martie, my children, and my friends if all through my life I didn't have the Spirit nudging me toward servanthood. Or I wonder how my lusts might have carried me down dead-end streets of grief masquerading as pleasure if God had not been teaching me self-control. What might greed have done if He had not tutored me in generosity? I shudder to think what all these years without Christ might have looked like.

If you ever think you haven't been forgiven much because of an early rescue in your life, think about what might have been. When that comes into clear view, you will have enough reason to love Him for the rest of your life and understand in a new way the words of a hymn, "Oh, to grace how great a debtor daily I'm constrained to be!"

When I think of what might have been, I know I owe Christ far more than I could ever repay.

When I think of what might have been, I know I owe Christ far more than I could ever repay.

Think as well of what He has kept from you today. First Corinthians 10:13 assures us that nothing comes into our lives for which He doesn't give us grace to carry or a way of escape. God is overseeing every aspect of our lives and stands like a guardian, keeping out all that would overwhelm and destroy us. And when we understand the hatred the devil has for us and the treachery of his schemes, we live in grateful worship to Christ for His protection. If we ever drop our heads on the pillow thinking, "Well, He didn't do much for me today," it means we have forgotten how busy and involved He has been. We should go to sleep every night with prayers of overflowing gratitude for what He did during the day that we know nothing about to shield and defend us.

So I have concluded that my street friends and others who have been radically transformed have nothing on me. I, too, am a debtor. In fact, the amazing grace bestowed on me in my being born into a godly home, getting an early start, and being shielded from much that would have harmed me gives me an even greater reason for loving Christ. Since when did I deserve this advantage?

Position

As the religious leader of his town, Simon was the living expression of what it means to be righteous and good. It would have been hard for him to believe in his own depravity when his public position trumpeted his own goodness.

Part of the territory that comes with doing what I do at Moody is that some people feel I must be a fairly good person to occupy such a position. Pastors, Bible teachers, church elders, philanthropists, and other people of profile and power in the kingdom of God all have the same problem. If we are not careful, we begin to believe that our position and the resultant affirmation are a true reflection of our standing before God.

Periodically I overhear someone whisper to a friend and point toward me, saying something like, "That's the president of Moody." Yet, if they knew what I know about myself, they would be less than impressed. I often remind myself that if it weren't for the position no one would give me a second glance. If our hearts and heads are unguarded, position can be an inebriating privilege. If we really believe that what it says on our business cards affirms our goodness, we are left with little except the shallow exercise of loving ourselves for what we do.

This had to be a part of Simon's struggle. How could he admit his need for a Savior and join this woman at Jesus' feet? People who did what he did were not the ones who needed saving. In fact it was their prerogative to sit in judgment on those who did. Simon's position as the lead religious guy in town put him at a great disadvantage when it came to understanding who Christ was and why he needed Him so desperately.

We should reflect on the fact that when some of God's highly positioned people came into His presence, they were struck with the depth of their sinfulness and their utter vulnerability before a holy God. Isaiah froze in his tracks as a dead man and immediately felt the pain of his sinfulness (Isa. 6:1–6). The apostle John fell before Christ in abject terror and fear (Rev. 1:17). Peter was shamed by his own sinfulness when he experienced Christ's miraculous power (Luke 5:8).

> *The sooner we understand that position is only a*
> *function assigned by God and not a barometer of*
> *our need, the quicker we will be able to love with*
> *the adoring gratitude He deserves.*

The sooner we understand that position is only a function assigned by God and not a barometer of our need before God, the quicker we will be able to love Him with the adoring gratitude He deserves.

The Point System

One of the great misconceptions among Christians is that the sin problem is about how many sins we commit. If this is indeed the issue, we can understand why Simon felt he didn't have to be forgiven much. His sin count would have been admirably low, on some days perhaps even zero. His problem—and ours—is that it is not the number of sins or the type of sins that so deeply offends God. It is the fact that *we are sinners* who from our mother's womb have been alienated and at war with Him (Eph. 2:1–10).

Most of us measure our sinfulness in one of two ways. One is that we count our sins and, in spite of the fact that we know we are not perfect, we feel we score pretty well. The second is that we play the comparison game by keeping other people's score and comparing theirs with ours. The old ploy of the Pharisees, "Lord, I thank you that I am not as others" (see Luke 18:11), never fails to bolster our sense of righteousness.

I am reminded of the man who upon arriving in heaven noticed that all the clocks had names under them. He asked Peter, who seemed to be the Q&A resource in heaven, "What's with all the clocks?" Peter answered that they were not clocks but "sin meters." He noticed that Billy Graham's hardly ever moved. The pope's seemed to be motionless as well. Other well-known people's meters moved very little. The man asked Peter, "Does Stowell have a clock?" To which Peter replied, "It's in the office. We use it as a fan."

Christ-lovers, understand: Our problem before a Holy God is not the amount of our sins but the fact that we *are* sinners and that within us lies the potential for every heinous sin in the book. We take great pride in our outrage toward the awful sins of movie stars, politicians, and other public figures. We wag our righteous fingers at those who consort with immorality. In our worst moments we foolishly take guarded delight in news that another Christian has become involved in a scandal. We feel so much better about ourselves knowing that they have departed and that we have remained true.

But it never seems to cross our minds that within each of us lies the potential for all those sins and more. We could be the rapists, the child abusers, and the serial killers of our world, if it weren't for the amazing grace of God in bringing us salvation. It is He who has given us good and godly homes, churches, and fellow followers to hold us accountable. If it weren't for the indwelling Spirit and the Word of God to guide, reprove, teach, and correct us, we may very well have been among the worst of them. We carry all the seeds of sin. The only difference is that we are now forgiven and reengineered. The difference is that we belong to that sub group known as the "forgiven-much."

If life to us is about counting our sins and comparing ourselves with other sinners, we will find it hard to adore our Savior. But if we realize that it is our own sinful ways that nailed Him to the cross, we will never recover from the impact of that kind of mercy.

I like the way the hymn writer puts it:

My sin—O the bliss of this glorious thought—
My sin, not in part, but the whole,
Is nailed to the cross, and I bear it no more:
Praise the Lord, praise the Lord, O my soul!

Until we recover an accurate view of our condition before God, we will never know how great His grace is, nor will our hearts acknowledge the debt we owe. Affectionate adoration is the response of a heart that needs to be and has been forgiven much. It ignites when we recognize the reality of our jeopardy before God and the inexhaustible grace and mercy He has shown us.

If you are tempted to think about a point system, then think of this: Jesus scored all the points on the cross and has benevolently put that victory in your account.

The test of whether or not we have gotten beyond our parentage, position, and keeping score comes in the daily routines and encounters of life. At the crossroads of a compelling temptation, do we stop to ask whether we love Him more than the temptation? When we hear His call to step out in radical, security-threatening acts of obedience, do we think of His radical life-threatening act of obedience on our behalf? Does the power of that thought propel us past the fears that loom on the edge of radical obedience? Lacking these impulses of a true Christ-lover leaves us with only shear discipline or imminent failure. Worse yet, I find that any success I experience from the mastery of the moment only fuels my sense of self-righteous pride which only drags my heart farther from the love-inducing sense of my deep indebtedness to Christ.

What will trigger this transition from a cold, calculated life of religious robotics to the authentic love that drives and defines all that we do?

The late songwriter Keith Green expressed well the cry of our hearts as we seek to love Christ after the model of this celebrated woman:

My eyes are dry,
My faith is old,
My heart is hard,
My prayers are cold,
And you know how I ought to be,
Alive to you and dead to me.

Is there a road back for us? Can a love for the divine be kindled in the hearts of hardened followers? How can we reclaim the affection that delivers us from the stale and sterile experience of a loveless faith? Is it possible to move from the seat of Simon to the side of the woman at the feet of Jesus?

Yes, it is possible. But it requires that we renew our minds to see ourselves as we really are. It requires that we deal with distorting issues like wanting to think well of ourselves and wrap our lives in image enhancing paraphernalia. It means that issues of parentage, position, and grading ourselves on the point system cannot disillusion us.

And once we have begun the process of liberation from deceptive views of ourselves, there will be one more ambush to face—our view of God. Like Simon, when we think too much of ourselves we of necessity end up thinking too little of God. When we get, as they used to say, too big for our britches, we have probably become too big to love Christ. The remedy to an oversized me? *Fear God.* It seems an unusual requirement to fear someone before you can love them. But that is exactly what Scripture says.

THE FEAR OF GOD IS THE BEGINNING

The Bible does not call us to love God because we are afraid of Him. Rather, we are to love Him because of the way in which He responds to us when we come face-to-face with His terrifying holiness.

*We won't be struck with awe and adoration until
we know the magnificence and terror of His being.*

Count on it, we won't be struck with awe and adoration until we know the magnificence and terror of His being. And we will never comprehend our wretched sinfulness until we have seen the blazing purity of His holiness. The dramatic contrast between our fallen frailty and God's perfect purity puts His tender mercy toward us in bold relief.

In Deuteronomy 6:1–5 God reveals the foundational way that Israel was to relate to Him. Three issues are put forward:

Fear the Lord
Affirm that He is the only God
Love the Lord your God with all your heart, soul, and strength.

As we have mentioned, fear and love are not normal companions in a thriving love relationship. We don't build healthy relationships by living in constant fear of the one we love. But if we are to turn our hearts toward loving Christ, we must cultivate a healthy sense of what the Bible calls "fearing God."

This kind of fearful love does not come easily in a world that encourages a small view of God.

Gone are the awe-inspiring cathedrals and the echoing sounds of great organs that draw our hearts to a transcendent God who is bigger than we are and worthy to be held in mysterious awe. Today we worship in comfortable, living-room-type churches that often seem to be man centered rather than God centered. We hear soothing messages of a God who lovingly accepts us and tolerates our whims and weaknesses. One pastor who has a global television ministry was recently quoted as saying,

> I don't think that anything has been done in the name of Christ and under the banner of Christianity that has proven more destructive to human personality, and hence counterproductive to the evangelistic enterprise, than the unchristian, uncouth strategy of attempting to make people aware of their lost and sinful condition.[1]

We are encouraged to see God as a companion who will fit into our "buddy system." As a wallet-sized God who serves us as a divine credit card to grant us every desire and impulse for personal gain. As the spiritual "911" number of our lives. As a passport across the great eternal divide. And then, when He doesn't perform to our desires, we get irritated and threaten to discard our faith.

Barbara Ehrenreich observes in an essay in *Time* magazine that "our desire to make the awesome adorable is spoiling the mysteries of life." Among her many examples of our tendency to "dumb down" the profound is the way NASA dubbed the rocks on its recent probe to Mars. They gave the stones names like Yogi, Scooby Doo, and Barnacle Bill—as though, Ehrenreich suggests, "Someone high up in NASA must have issued a firm directive: 'Keep it cuddly, guys. . . .'"[2]

I was hoping the author wouldn't notice how our modern brand of Christianity has trivialized the God that we should hold in awe, respect, and adoration. Much to my dismay, she did notice.

> Watch one of those shlockier televangelists, and you'll be introduced to an affable deity eager to be enlisted as your personal genie. Yes, the Great Spinner of Galaxies, Digger of Black Holes is available, for a suitable "love offering," to relieve the itch of hemorrhoids and help you prevail in office intrigues!

She notes with poignant insight,

> At least the ancient Hebrews had the good sense to make Yahweh unnamable and unseeable except in the flames of the burning bush—a permanent mystery.[3]

Until we see God in His terrifying size and limitless scope, we will never see ourselves as we really are. Nor will we lovingly appreciate the fact that a God like this chose to love you and me. We must ask the question the little girl asked her dad upon watching planes fly overhead and seeing them get smaller and smaller as they climbed into the sky. When she finally took a plane trip with her family, she grew increasingly pensive and asked her father, "Are we small yet?"

Until we see God in His terrifying size and limitless scope, we will never see ourselves as we really are.

Seeing Him as He is, we sense our overwhelming vulnerability in the face of His holy perfection and unlimited power. It is in the context of His expansive reality, and this context alone, that we see ourselves as we really are: small, defenseless, weak, guilty, and deserving of His judgment. Jerome Miller puts it,

> Standing before what I experience as ultimately Sacred, I myself am compelled to acknowledge that in and of myself I am precisely nothing. Before the Sacred, I feel, in and of myself, utterly insignificant, utterly without substance. I cannot take myself seriously.

He notes that the only response we can have in the face of God is . . .

> Terror, which is itself fear rendered acute and panicky by an imminent danger, has, of course, always been recognized as an appropriate response to the Sacred.[4]

When was the last time you thought of God in these terms?

We have long forgotten that even our good works in the light of His holy presence are like filthy rags (Isa. 64:6). Why do we still parade them as a badge of honor in His presence? I tend to assume that He would be impressed if I could take Him through all that I have done as a husband, a father, a pastor, and the president of Moody Bible Institute. You and I could point out all the times we have said no to temptation and said yes to the really hard things He has asked us to do. But He is not impressed. Under the damning spotlight of His pure holiness we are left with nothing and can only say with the songwriter, "Nothing in my hand I bring, simply to Thy cross I cling."

Any thoughts that upon seeing Him we might hug Him, high-five Him, or query Him with a list of nagging theological questions are shamefully ridiculous notions. As we have noted, both the prophet Isaiah and the apostle John were rendered immobile with fright when they encountered God. Isaiah immediately saw his sinfulness and the sinfulness of the nation, and John fell as a dead man at His feet.

Defenseless, we too must fall at His feet, terrorized in the presence of the radiant purity, size, and scope of His being, and repentantly beg for His mercy.

And when we do, something unexpected and wonderful happens.

Instead of annihilating us, which we readily acknowledge we deserve, He reaches out in love and touches us with cleansing grace. He adopts us as His children, grants us an inheritance, and offers us unlimited access to His presence. He fills our trembling hearts with hope, confidence, and courage and promises ultimately to deliver us to an eternity of unlimited joy and pleasure in His presence.

When we see Him as He really is, we become convinced that all we really need is Him and the grace He gives. The grace that cancels His wrath even in the face of our greatest offenses. The grace that gives us an edge over all that would destroy us. Knowing Him, we find our hearts growing in adoring love, not with ourselves or the works of our hands, but with Him—Him and Him alone. And we sense deep down inside that this is the way it should be, the way it should have been all along.

> *When we see Him as He really is, He assures us that all we really need is Him and the grace He gives.*

Christ-lovers never lose sight of the wonder of His greatness and the appropriate sense of terror in His presence. Nor do Christ-lovers ever forget the touch of His healing grace and rescuing mercy, the grace and mercy that transformed His hand of wrath to a touch of redemptive recovery. The tender touch that brought peace to our trembling, troubled hearts. For this our hearts are filled with unquenchable affection and adoration, forever.

FROM SLUDGE TO SERVICE

For centuries the Stradivarius violin was a mystery. Why would just one violin maker be able to do what no one else has done before or since, particularly since he was poor and could not afford the best woods of his day? Recent studies have began to answer the question. The prevailing theory is that Stradivarius took most of the wood from the polluted harbor where he lived. This wood had been soaked in the sludge of the harbor for years. It was the choice wood that had been used to make oars, boats, and other seaworthy instruments. Broken and abandoned in the harbor, the wood had fallen victim to the decay-infested microbes in the pollutants.

Studies of the wood used in Stradivarius violins show that these microbes ate the cells of the wood hollow, leaving only the infrastructure of the cells to remain. In the hand of Stradivarius, these thousands of hollow chambers in each piece of wood were transformed from worthless empty spaces into resonating cathedrals of sound with every pull of the bow. Stradivarius rescued worthless scraps of wood, hopelessly damaged and drifting in a polluted environment, and used them to enrich our world with a beauty found nowhere else.

We are all, even the best of us, like the wood. Broken, abandoned and lost in the sludge of sin. And, by an incomprehensible act of the great God of the universe, we have been rescued and transformed. The hand of the Master Redeemer has crafted us into an instrument of unique beauty. The hollow cells that sin carved within us now resonate life sounds that glorify Christ and we in turn fill our world with the unsurpassed priceless harmony of His presence in us and through us. Who of us can help but say to the woman, "Excuse me, but could I kneel beside you to tell Him how much I love Him as well?"

CHAPTER SEVEN

"DO YOU LOVE ME?"

Staying on Mission

The maturing process of the male species can be measured by the kind of stores we enjoy browsing in. As a child, I liked toy stores. During my teens, sports stores held my interest, where the highest joy was trying on baseball gloves, getting the feel of a bat, or handling a football. In college, clothing stores caught my attention as I was determined to look "cool." Then, as a young husband and father, it was electronic stores, where I could envision filling our home with the richest sounding music with the very best woofers and tweeters available.

But as men we go our separate ways. Those who are maturing with great intellectual capacity will spend the rest of their years wandering through bookstores. If we enjoy pastimes like golf, tennis, and fishing, then it's back to the sports stores for the rest of our lives.

And while I enjoy bookstores, *my* maturing processes have resulted in a new and growing love for hardware stores. Gadgets galore intrigue and tempt me. I can identify with the guy wearing the T-shirt that says, "He who dies with the most tools wins." Fortunately—or unfortunately—there is a mega-hardware store in our neighborhood that is open twenty-four hours a day. Late one evening, I had to get a part for one of my projects.

As I roamed the aisles, I passed by a massive display of light switches. Since some of the remodeling under way at home would require switches, I stopped to survey the vast variety available. I was taken with a particular kind of rheostat that has a row of LED lights that disclose exactly how bright or dim one has set the light. With a simple touch the lights go brighter or dimmer according to the preset command. By contrast, the old-fashioned rheostats were a round knob that had to be punched in and turned to the correct setting each time. The high-tech rheostats had captured my heart—I couldn't wait for them to be installed.

When the time came to obtain the switches, I told Martie about the great advances in rheostats and how nice they would be in place of the old kind. After my eloquent description, she simply said, "I really like the old kind. You can get any kind you want, but regular rheostats would make me happy." My dreams were dashed, but off I went, knowing that she had given me a small window of permission to do what I wanted to do.

As I stood by the display, a war of sorts raged in my heart. I could get what I wanted . . . it wouldn't do irreparable damage to the relationship . . . or I could make a love statement to Martie and get the switches that would please her.

I bought the switches Martie wanted.

I learned a long time ago that loving means caring about the things that the one I love cares about. True love gives up personal interests for the needs and desires of the one I claim to love. While I don't always love so selflessly, on this occasion love won the day.

DO YOU LOVE ME?

This truth has huge ramifications for those who want to develop a growing love for Christ. He knows He is loved when what is important to Him is important to us. It is this dynamic of love that drives the troubling question Jesus poses to Peter—not once, but three times—in the last recorded conversation Jesus has with him. "Simon son of

John, do you truly love me more than these?" And then twice more, "Do you truly love me?" "Do you love me?" (John 21:15–17).

Christ knows He is loved when what is important to Him is important to us.

When someone you are supposed to love asks, "Do you love me?" it is a pretty good sign that something has gone wrong in the relationship. For Jesus to ask that question of Peter is especially troubling, since it singles him out in front of a group of other disciples and puts Peter on the spot.

Peter's response comes quickly: "Yes, Lord, you know that I love you."

For centuries scholars have debated the significance of Peter's words, trying to discover whether Peter really did love Christ—as though the words one uses are the true test of our love. When Jesus asks Peter the love question, He uses the word *agape.* This word is the willful commitment to love regardless of feeling or circumstances. We have been schooled to believe that "agape" love is the deepest and most certain kind of love, since it is the word used to express God's unconditional love to us. So when Peter responds to Jesus using the word *phileo,* which means familial love between brothers or close friends, we assume that he is saying that he does not love Jesus as deeply as he should. We then assume that the reason Jesus continues to query Peter is to try to upgrade his response to an "agape" kind of love.

I really don't think the point of the text lies in the words being used. In the first place, in the last of His three questions, Jesus used the word *phileo* himself when he questioned Peter. It would seem way out of character for Jesus to concede to a lesser kind of love from Peter or anyone else; He never negotiates deals when it comes to our commitment to Him. Second, it is possible that Peter uses the word *phileo* to indicate that his love for Jesus is actually more than a commitment of the will. He might be saying, "Lord, you know that I love you as I would a brother. We have an intense three-year history to our relationship, and we have bonded in many ways. My love for you runs deeper than mere commitment!" It would not be like Peter to stand on ceremony when it comes to verbalizing his commitment to Christ. It is more probable that he wants to take Jesus' question the extra mile.

The point that Jesus is making is not a quibbling over words. Rather, He presses the issue that if Peter really loves Him, then Peter will be interested in and committed to the things that He is interested in and committed to.

If Peter loves Christ, then the proof of his love will be his commitment to the spiritual needs and nurture of people as the highest priority of his life. Or, in Jesus' words, "Tend My lambs. . . . Shepherd My sheep. . . . Tend My sheep" (John 21:15–17 NASB).

When we married, I soon realized that Martie has a deep love for animals in general and dogs in particular. She grew up with Trudy, a black lab, who was a faithful friend and companion. I grew up in a home that never placed much value on pets. So I brought a well-intentioned disinterest to the marriage. It is not that my parents hadn't tried. We had a parakeet, but it is difficult to bond with birds. A onetime run with a puppy didn't last long, because no one took up the task of caring for him. One Easter someone gave us some round furry yellow chicks—only to have my sister accidentally step on one as it ran across the kitchen floor. So in all my growing up years, pets had not scored big with me.

I soon became aware that my disinterest and Martie's deep affection for things with fur created a distance between us. It wasn't quite like "Love me, love my dog," but almost. An important part of loving her would be to love what she loves. So we bought a dog. (And I walked the dog. And I fed the dog.)

Christ's passion is people. He knows that everything will be checked at the border of eternity except for people. He rescues, stabilizes, and strengthens people for life here and eternity there. As strange as it seems at first, He claimed to be God, but loved tax collectors even though they were the scorn of everyone else. He embraced sinners, seeking Pharisees, rich and poor, Samaritans and prostitutes. People—all of them—were Christ's highest priority and the focus of His deep compassion. On one occasion He looked out on the masses and, as Matthew puts it, "When he saw the crowds, he had compassion on them, because they were harassed and helpless, like sheep without a shepherd" (Matt. 9:36). Which then prompted Him to tell the disciples to pray that there would be enough workers to bring the good news to alleviate the suffering and despair.

At His triumphal entry, on what we celebrate as Palm Sunday, Christ's heart was not on His well-deserved yet rare public recognition as King but rather on the needs of the people. Luke records that as He approached Jerusalem, Jesus saw the city and wept (Luke 19:41).

And if there is any doubt that Jesus was totally absorbed in the eternal and spiritual needs of people, then one journey to the foot of the cross resolves the debate. He didn't die for a political cause or for some stubborn personal agenda. He willingly died for people—for you, for me.

> *With Christ, in a very real sense, it is "Love me, love my people."*

So He presses Peter to show his love for Him, not by the words he uses, but by the place that people hold in his life. With Christ, in a very real sense, it is "Love me, love my people."

TRUE COMMITMENT

Martie and I recently took a twelve-day ministry trip to Hong Kong during which we spent time with many fascinating people. I spent part of one evening with a Moody graduate who was on a brief furlough from his ministry in the Philippines. He and his Chinese wife and two small children, one of whom has Down's syndrome, are church planting among the poorest of the poor in the slums of Manila. Another Moody graduate, whose husband died suddenly after just a few years of marriage, had stayed in Hong Kong as a missionary. She was on her way to Mongolia (on an airline that serves yak as the entrée) to spend a week with some other missionaries, to be a resource and encouragement to them.

We had lunch with Dave and Theresa Magee. They and their two teenage children had only been in Hong Kong for three months. Dave left a lucrative legal career in Chicago, attended seminary, then became the pastor of an English-speaking church in Hong Kong. We also met a veteran missionary couple who have served Christ in Hong Kong for over thirty-five years. They told us they were ready to retire from the mission. When we asked what they would do after retirement they beamed to tell us they were going to go into mainland China to plant a church.

Somehow, it seems to me that Christ knows He is loved deeply by people like these. They are driven by what drives Him, and they are committed to what He is committed to.

A pastor friend recently told me of a couple in his church who, deciding they had made enough money, sold everything to open an AIDS clinic to reach out in Christ's name to some of the neediest people. In the same conversation he mentioned a businessman in his church who turned down a lucrative and much-sought-after promotion because it meant the amount of travel would take him away from his children too much of the time.

Not all of us will be called to such radical and risky expressions of love for Christ, but He still is always interested in our love for Him. A quick glance at our Daytimer, checkbook ledger, or social calendar will probably reveal quite accurately whether Christ would be forced to ask us the question He asked Peter.

BEHIND THE QUESTIONS

The fact that Jesus confronts Peter in such a direct and demanding way indicates that He might suspect that Peter doesn't love Him as much as he should. Just asking the question suggests that there is a problem. If your spouse meets you at the door as you come home and in serious tones looks in your eyes and asks, "Do you love me? I really need to know if you love me," you immediately know something is wrong.

And in this scene with Peter, something is. The real story behind the triple quiz lies not within the words but rather in the reason Jesus had to ask the questions in the first place. When we discover what went wrong in Peter's life, we discover what may be wrong in ours as well.

Earlier in the story, Peter tells a group of the disciples he is going fishing (John 21:3). It becomes clear that he is not talking about a day off to relax on the other end of a fishing pole. Jesus would not censure Peter for that, for He often went off by Himself to rest awhile. We need space to replenish our souls when we become weary.

What Peter is saying to Nathaniel, James, John, and the others is that he is going back to life as it had been before he met Jesus—to a career in fishing. The other disciples agree and get into the boats with Peter. James and John knew the drill well, for they too had been fishermen before Jesus called them to His ministry.

This was Peter's second major failure. After three years of following Jesus, he was going back to life as usual. For him the gig was up and he would now go off mission, off calling, and off message and return to his previous interests and energies.

While a lot of press is given to Peter's betrayal less than a month earlier, little attention seems to focus on this backtracking in his life. Yet, in some respects this could be the most serious of his failures. Not that his betrayal of Christ was not a serious sin—it was. But it was so wrong that it immediately caught the attention of Peter's heart, and he was filled with sorrow. The treachery in this second failure is that Peter might assume that this switch back to his earlier life is hardly a problem.

It is the subtlety of this move that is so frightening. In one sense, the consequences of Peter's "return-to-life-as-usual" move are far more detrimental to his life than his denial. If Peter reneges on Jesus' calling in his life, who will speak so convincingly at the feast of Pentecost? Who

LOVING CHRIST

will carry the gospel to the Gentiles? Who will find hope that impetuous, vacillating, unsteady people can be greatly used of God?

In fairness to Peter, we must admit that it is not hard to understand why he is ready to go off mission at this point in his life. First, he undoubtedly is disappointed and confused about what Jesus is up to now that His death and resurrection have taken place. Peter has seen Jesus only twice since the resurrection, and then only in brief encounters, as when He showed up through locked doors (John 20:19, 26). For three years Peter was close to Jesus, caught up in the crescendoing popularity of His leader. Peter had often stepped out in front of the others to do whatever Jesus wanted.

Now everything has changed. Peter doesn't know where Jesus is staying or what He is doing between His rare, brief appearances. Waiting uninformed in the wings, hoping that maybe something big will break, goes against every fiber of Peter's impetuous nature. Not only is he disappointed and confused, but his material needs also loom largely in front of him. Where will he get food to eat? How will he buy the clothes he will soon need? After all, that scoundrel Judas absconded with all the funds. Peter had always trusted Jesus for these things—but now it is time to fend for himself.

So, disappointed and distracted by earthly needs, he and the others decide to go back to the nets they had so willingly left three years ago.

Scripture tells us that they fish all night and catch nothing (John 21:5). Now, I guess it's all right to get "skunked," as my dad used to say, if you are on vacation. But if it's your first day back in business and you catch nothing, it's a big deal.

There has to be a sense of disillusionment setting in as the darkness gives way to the early morning light. Realizing that their best-laid plans and long, hard efforts have been to no avail, Peter and the others are missing the sense of excitement they used to feel when they hauled in nets full of fish.

There is a pattern here that needs to catch our attention. Our plans for advancing our own destinies and prosperity, if they are not driven by our calling in Christ, always end up as empty, disillusioning pursuits.

So this first night back to their career is far spent, the disciples are exhausted, the sea is glassed by the early morning calm, and the seven used-to-be followers of Jesus have to be quietly wondering why their nets are empty. As the light breaks, do the hillsides that cascade down to the water's edge remind them of the time Jesus fed the five thousand on these hills and of how hungry they are becoming? Do they wonder what they will do after investing nearly three years of their lives with the Messiah? If that is what is occupying their minds, they don't have to wonder much longer.

As the early morning haze that wraps the shore begins to lift, Jesus appears on the beach and calls out, "Friends, you do not have any fish, do you?" (Jesus never asks questions because He doesn't know the answer; He asks questions to get people's attention and drive a point home.) Not recognizing this person, the disciples answer that the assumption is correct—they have caught nothing. He then says, "Cast the net on the right-hand side of the boat, and you will find a catch." They follow His recommendation and cannot haul the fish in because the catch is so great.

John turns to Peter and says, "It is the Lord!"

When Peter realizes who it is, he throws his robe on and jumps into the sea to swim to meet Jesus—a typical Peter move as he leaves the rest of the crew to fight their way to the shore, dragging their now strained nets bulging with fish.

One wonders why Peter was so quick to go overboard to meet Christ.

This has to be a very poignant moment for Peter. This scenario had happened once before. Interestingly enough, it was this exact kind of miracle that led to his call to follow Jesus and fish for men in the first place (Luke 5:1–11). At that time, as Jesus was teaching, the crowd was pressing Him closer and closer to the sea. He asked some fishermen if they would row Him out into the sea so He can teach away from the press of the crowd. They gladly comply. One of them was Peter. When Jesus had finished teaching, He said to the fishermen, "Put out into deep water, and let down the nets for a catch." They replied that they had fished all night and had caught nothing, but, nevertheless, they would do as He said. Upon letting their nets down, they caught so many fish that their nets began to break and their boat began to sink.

Peter was so struck with the authority and power of Christ that he fell down at Jesus' feet and said, "Go away from me, Lord! I am a sinful man!" But Jesus reassured Simon, "Don't be afraid; from now on you will catch men." And then he and his friends brought their boats to land and left everything and followed Him.

There isn't a chance in the world that Peter doesn't remember the stunning encounter he had with Jesus three years earlier. And it is no coincidence that Jesus finds Peter, on the very night he has decided to go back to being a fisherman, and replicates the miracle. Jesus is graphically confronting Peter with the moment of his call. To Peter, who has just gone off calling and off mission, this encounter reminds him of the day he gave up everything to follow Jesus. And we have to ask Peter, "What has changed? Has the calling changed? Has Jesus changed? Or have you changed?" If Peter had been disappointed with Jesus yesterday, this encounter changes all of that. Jesus still loves him. Jesus still calls him. And Peter runs to shore to meet Him.

Amid your disappointments and thoughts that Jesus has given up on you—discover that He hasn't. At just the right time He will meet and reassure you.

Amid your disappointments and thoughts that Jesus has given up on you—discover that He hasn't. At just the right time He will meet and reassure you. He has not changed, nor has His calling for your life to be focused on the spiritual needs and nurture of people changed.

MEET HIM FOR BREAKFAST

As Peter reaches the shore, he sees that Jesus has built a charcoal fire on which He is cooking fish for their breakfast (John 21:9). You have heard of the Last Supper—well, this is the last breakfast, and for Peter it may be equally important.

I can't help but wonder if Peter doesn't remember the last time he was around a charcoal fire. It was that terrible moment when he denied his Lord. Smells have a way of triggering memories: your mother's perfume, the burning of leaves in the fall. Does the smell of the burning charcoal remind Peter of his previous failure to be faithful to Christ? My guess is that Peter is reminded afresh with the smell of the fire that Jesus meets us in our failures in order to restore us to a loving pursuit of our calling.

The lesson in this breakfast is profound and necessary for all of us who are tempted to take life off calling and go back to a more comfortable, more predictable routine. As Peter and the others come to shore, Jesus is already cooking the fish for breakfast. Where did He get the fish? In this quiet miracle of the story lies a lesson that both Peter and we need to learn.

The lesson is simply this: God has the ability, the interest, and the love to provide for our needs, miraculously if necessary. And God is often pleased to provide in generous and abundant ways. Not only does Christ have fish already cooking on shore, but when the disciples count their catch, they notice that there are so many fish that the net should have broken. And they are large fish—153 of them, to be exact! Jesus has prepared a big enough breakfast so that seven hardworking, up-all-night fishermen have plenty to go around. As F. B. Meyer so wonderfully points out, with God it is always the fatted calf, the best robe, and the ring. With Him, our cup "runneth over"!

Jesus wants the disciples to know that He will gladly manage the supply in their lives, and that for them to leave the important work of the kingdom to create their own financial security is a serious mistake.

Jesus could have called them all to shore, sat them down, and lectured them about their lame approach to life. Instead, He graciously and lovingly illustrates His point by supplying their needs. He will manage their hunger. He will manage the income they need to live. And, once they get a grip on this reality, they will be free to give themselves to the work of Christ.

Of course, Jesus had tried to teach them this before. One time the disciples were ready to go off vision because their shoes, robes, and stomachs were having a problem. After telling about a man who wanted his brother to divide the inheritance with him, Jesus turned to the crowd and said, "Watch out! Be on your guard against all kinds of greed; a man's life does not consist in the abundance of his possessions" (Luke 12:15). No doubt the disciples liked the way Jesus got in the face of this man who cared more about money than relationships and contentment. But then He turned to them and reproved them because their own worries were threatening their commitment to Him. If God didn't care about their needs, they would have had good reason to bail out just to survive. But Jesus noted that God does see their needs and He does lovingly provide. Poignantly Jesus told the distracted disciples,

> "Therefore I tell you, do not worry about your life, what you will eat; or about your body, what you will wear. Life is more than food, and the body more than clothes. Consider the ravens: They do not sow or reap, they have no storeroom or barn; yet God feeds them. And how much more valuable you are than birds! . . .
>
> "Consider how the lilies grow. They do not labor or spin. Yet I tell you, not even Solomon in all his splendor was dressed like one of these. If that is how God clothes the grass of the field, which is here today, and tomorrow is thrown into the fire, how much more will he clothe you, O you of little faith! And do not set your heart on what you will eat or drink; do not worry about it. For the pagan world runs after all such things. . . ."

Jesus concludes,

> ". . . and your Father knows that you need them. But seek his kingdom, and these things will be given to you as well.
> "Do not be afraid, little flock, for your Father has been pleased to give you the kingdom" (Luke 12:22–32).

Peter is oblivious to the fact that the greatest victories of the kingdom have been won while he is worrying about what is going to happen to him. Sin has been dealt a fatal and eternal blow. Satan's cruelest weapon, death, has been conquered by the resurrection. And the world is soon to receive the liberating power of the gospel through people who are filled with the Holy Spirit. It has just been a matter of days, but it is too long for Peter. So he concludes that he has to get on with his life on his terms.

It is often in quiet times like these, when He seems far away, that God does His greatest work, preparing people for the strategic things that lie just ahead.

It is often in quiet times like these, when He seems far away, that God does His greatest work, preparing people for the strategic things that lie just ahead. Loving Christ is about staying on calling even when nothing dramatic is going on. It is not about bailing out when prayers seem unanswered, when life has come to a screeching halt, when what has happened is not at all what we have expected God to do, when life is tougher and less rewarding than we thought, when others who turn to their own agendas prosper while we continue to be faithful. It is only an unshakable belief that Christ will not disappoint us in the end that keeps us on calling during the silent seasons of life.

At just the right time Christ breaks the silence. As He meets the disciples in the midst of their new endeavors, He teaches them the principle of "supply-side spirituality." That principle is, "You worry about the spiritual needs of people, and I will worry about the needs of your life." This is not to say that we must immediately leave our jobs and become unemployed in the morning, although for a few of us our calling may mean just that. It does mean that we do not live or work for our own agendas. Christ-loving followers make the eternal destinies and spiritual growth of people the end, the goal, of all that they do.

For us, this may mean doing a great job at work, not for our own promotion, but so that others will know that Christ is in the business of making trustworthy productive people. It will mean figuring out how much we need to live on and then prayerfully looking for ways to give the rest away in order to advance the work of the kingdom. It may mean that when our children feel called to serve the Lord in their careers, we celebrate the high honor of having their passions focused on work that is so dear to Christ's heart. It may be about taking our professional skills to some faraway land and sacrificing time and income to assist the work of Christ that desperately needs what we have to offer. We do this because we trust that Christ will meet our needs if we put His interests and passions first in life. He is always there for us and won't let us down. So trust in Him. He will be sure to do His part.

It was because Peter had bailed out on Jesus that Jesus asks him, "Do you love me?" And now the story comes full circle. He turns to Peter after He has fixed and fed them breakfast and says, "Do you love me more than these?" One might assume that Jesus is asking Peter to contrast the quality of his love for Him with the love the other disciples have for Him. But frankly, that is an unlikely spin on the passage. First, it hardly seems probable that Jesus would press Peter into the comparison game in front of the other followers. Second, it really does not fit the context.

Then what does Jesus mean?

With the pile of slippery, smelly fish flopping on the shore, Jesus is saying to Peter, who has left his spiritual calling for fish, "Do you love me more than you love these fish?" And, "if you do, the proof of your love will be that you rejoin Me in the far greater enterprise of being interested in what I am interested in—a world full of needy people as lost as lambs without a shepherd."

The lure of life-as-usual, life on its own terms, had seduced Peter off mission, off calling, and off message. Jesus made it perfectly clear that whatever Peter invested his life in would reflect his love—or lack of love—for Christ.

Perhaps you came to Christ with a heart eager to do anything and everything for Him. But slowly you have drifted back to the way life was before—except that you still attend church and serve on a committee or two. Yet, upon close examination you realize that it is not the spiritual needs and nurture of people that drives your agenda. It is still the old paradigm that life is primarily about you: what you can make, how much you can save, where you can retire, what your social life looks like, and where your golf handicap is going.

Jesus makes an interesting and convicting point. When He asks Peter if he loves Him more than the fish, He asks a question that would shame any of us. Will we love the fish or Jesus? The value statement in that question is shattering, even to the most hardened conscience. What are the fish in your life? Your career . . . money . . . a hobby . . . dreams . . . a relationship . . . a house? Anything that takes us off calling is a love affair with the wrong thing. Our love for Christ is proven in the reality of a life that loves what He loves.

When He walks through the things of your life and approaches your heart, I wonder if He sees a sign hung there on the door: GONE FISHIN'.

He wants to talk with you about the needs and nurture of people. Meet Him for breakfast.

CHAPTER EIGHT

THE GOOD NEIGHBOR POLICY

So Who Is My Neighbor?

I have written before about the morning I was commuting into Chicago while listening to the Brooklyn Tabernacle Choir at the highest volume from my car's tape deck. Driving alone, I was singing along as loud as I could and was totally enraptured in one of those rare seasons of worship that come from the deepest parts of your soul. On that day, my car was like a mobile temple. As I neared the city, the sun was rising in a haze behind the cityscape, pushing orange beams through the narrow slices of space between the buildings. Struck by the power and beauty of it all, I found my heart rejoicing because the God who was putting on this early-morning display of creation was the God who cares for me.

I pulled up to a traffic light, and facing me across the intersection was a cab with its left blinker on, inching forward against the red light. It was evident what he was planning in his wicked heart: He wanted to beat me through the intersection!

Because I was deep in worship, you might think I would give him the benefit of a doubt, and consider that perhaps a woman about to give birth had called him or that he was late for breakfast after a long night of work on the streets of Chicago, and therefore kindly yield the space to him.

I am ashamed to admit it, but as soon as the light turned green I nailed the accelerator and took off to guarantee that he didn't take advantage of me. He did the same and made a U-turn, missing my front fender by inches. We were now heading in the same direction and soon were sitting at the next red light beside each other. The problem with us as followers of Christ is that we don't have enough gestures to use in a time like this, so all I could do was throw both hands in the air as if to say, "What do you think you are doing?" as the choir continued to sing. . . .

My failure was more than a failure of love and mercy toward the cabby. In that moment I had failed to love Christ because He knows that we love Him by our love for the needs of people. Or as He said in another context, If you love me, love your neighbor (Matt. 22:34–40).

But then . . . maybe a cab driver is not my neighbor. He certainly does not live next door.

Then again . . .

Christ knows we love Him by watching what we do with our lives. And as unsettling as it may seem, how we treat people is the first place He looks.

When a lawyer asks Jesus, "What is the greatest commandment?" He answers that we are to love God with the totality of our being. But what He says next adds some definition. Although it was more than the scheming lawyer had asked for, Jesus adds the second most important command: "Love your neighbor as yourself" (Matt. 22:39). Jesus knows that we really can't have one without the other. Ironically, the Pharisees would have prided themselves in mastering their love for God but would be dreadfully lacking in loving their neighbor—which, in Jesus' book, would make the first command null and void.

Jesus underscores that the two commands are inseparably entwined when He calls this the "second" command. He does not mean second as inferior to or less important than the first, but rather, second in sequence. The point Jesus is making is this: "If you are gratefully surrendered to Me, then job number one is to love your neighbor." To which we might be tempted to reply, "Lord, you obviously have never met my neighbor! Could we talk about this? I'd be glad to double tithe, send my kids to bug-infested Africa, or even work in the nursery at church!"

He would be unimpressed with the offer. With gentle determination Jesus would remind us that our attitudes and actions toward others prove our love for God.

In fact, these two commands are so comprehensive that Jesus says the entire law stands or falls on them. And that, on reflection, makes sense. If we truly care about our neighbors' welfare, we would never lie to them to gain personal advantage. If we really love someone, we wouldn't covet that person's husband or wife or anything else he or she owns. Such sins as adultery and murder are out of the question if we are focused on the benefit and welfare of our neighbor.

That brings us back to the Pharisees' problem. They felt they fully understood the dynamics of loving God but often debated the issue of who their neighbor really was. In so doing, they argued away most of their responsibility to love others, particularly if the others were the "sinners" in town—the tax collectors, the Samaritans, or for sure, rude cab drivers!

This is why one of the experts in the law who is on the scene asks Jesus, "Who is my neighbor?" Jesus' response is wonderfully instructive; it sets the stage for Him to tell the story of the Good Samaritan. But before we expose our treatment of others to that story, another key question must be asked. If I am to love my neighbor as myself, what does it mean to love myself? If we are clear about this, we will have a clue as to how to love our neighbor.

Jesus acknowledges that certain aspects of loving ourselves are legitimate. In fact, nowhere in Scripture are we instructed to hate or despise ourselves. This is not a license to live selfishly as though we are the most important people in the universe, nor to stop caring for the needs of others. It simply reiterates that some of our instincts are focused inward naturally and productively.

Sometime ago I was trying to repair the family hair dryer. As you know, we are all victims of an international conspiracy that doesn't build appliances for well-meaning, ordinary husbands to fix. Determined to beat the system, I went after it anyway. The only way I could reach the screw that was sunk deeply into the plastic cover was to take my old pocketknife and put the skinny blade down the shaft. As I put pressure on the blade in an effort to engage and turn the screw, the pocketknife folded, squeezing my finger between itself and the sharp edge of the blade. My finger then had a rather bloody problem.

My first response was not, "Sorry, I don't have time to take care of you!" Rather, all my attention turned from the important repair job to the need of my finger. I yelled to Martie, and she came running, with the kids not far behind. She ran some water in the sink to wash the blood off and to stop the bleeding. I begged her not to run the water too cold . . . or too hot. When the kids pulled out the Band-Aids, I asked that we not cover too many hairs, since I knew it would be torturous to take it off. It was a classic example of self-love—fully attentive, tender, and eager.

The first test of the authenticity of love for Christ is measured by whether we treat our neighbors as though they were us.

In essence, our neighbor is to be the recipient of the same favor and grace that we show to ourselves. And the first test of the authenticity of love for Christ is measured by whether we treat our neighbors as though they were us.

THE GOOD NEIGHBOR

This brings us back to Jesus' answer to the question, "Who is my neighbor?" Jesus tells the familiar tale of a man who was mercilessly beaten, robbed, and left to die in the ditch by a band of ruthless thugs.

The road from Jerusalem to Jericho is about sixteen miles long and in that day was known as one of the most dangerous stretches of territory in the entire region. The terrain provided many rock formations for thieves to hide behind and then flee in afterward. Everyone listening to Jesus knew well the dangers of this road.

Jesus says that a man was traveling that road when he fell among thieves, who stripped him of everything, beat him into unconsciousness, and left him for dead by the roadside. Then two prominent, upstanding members of Jewish religious society—a priest and a Levite—came by, the first travelers to come upon the dying victim.

We are surprised, given our twenty-first-century mindset, that each walked by. We would expect far more of truly religious people. So we usually conclude that they were too busy with appointments and business in Jericho to take the time to stop. For that reason we wag our condemning finger to point out how easy it is for good folk to become messed up in their priorities.

But any Jews listening to the story would understand very well that their system of righteousness demanded that these men distance themselves from the traveler. For a priest to come within ten yards of a corpse would have made him ceremonially defiled, which in turn would disqualify him from performing priestly duties for two weeks. Even getting close enough to discern whether the man was dead or alive posed a serious risk to his purity.

Jesus' listeners would assume that the dying man was a Jew, because He said he was traveling from Jerusalem to Jericho. But the priest would not have had a clue. For all the priest knew, the man could be from the enemy territory of Samaria, and that alone would disqualify him as a legitimate object of love. So we can see why the priest actually stayed as far away from the victim as possible. In the priest's mind, it was the righteous thing to do—which should give all of us pause about systems of righteousness that blind our hearts and minds to the needs of fellow humans.

The Levite, no doubt having seen how the priest responded, would have excused himself because of the priest's example. While he was not bound by the same laws of defilement, the Levite would want to be as proper as the priest.

The important dynamic in this story is not that these two men were coldhearted, busy, or insensitive—as we usually conclude. It is rather that *they* were the *true* victims. They were victims of a view of the law and righteousness so distorted that it disabled them from keeping the law's most fundamental commands . . . to care about the needs of people.

Then Jesus, the master storyteller, turns the tale in an unexpected direction. He introduces a Samaritan. And what the Samaritan did would come as a total surprise. If you were Jewish and telling the story instead of Jesus, you might report that the Samaritan saw the victim and finished him off.

It is an understatement to say that Samaritans and Jews despised each other. Their mutual hatred stretched back for generations. They had ransacked each other's temples. From childhood the people on both sides were taught to have nothing to do with each other. Who can forget the utter amazement and shock of the disciples when they saw Jesus speaking with a woman of Samaria (John 4)? So the Samaritan Jesus introduces into the story has all the makings of a real villain.

Christ is defining neighbor *in a way that extends across religious, ethnic, and class lines. Our neighbor is any victim of life—regardless.*

Then, to everyone's surprise Jesus paints the Samaritan as the superhero. He takes pity on the victim, cares for him, and provides the means to see him safely restored to health. The actions of the Samaritan stand in bold contrast to the religious Jews who passed up the opportunity to love for the sake of preserving their perception of the law.

The point is that Christ is defining *neighbor* in a way that extends across religious, ethnic, and class lines. Our neighbor is any victim of life—regardless.

The Samaritan's heroic actions are also noteworthy because Jesus is saying that the most unlikely people—people outside our own religious systems—are often better at loving others than we are. Why? Because they are not bound by the prejudices we have imposed on ourselves.

Jesus then asks the questioner at the end of the story, "Which of these three do you think was a neighbor to the man who fell into the hands of robbers?" To which the lawyer responds, "The one who had mercy on him." Jesus adds, "Go and do likewise" (Luke 10:36–37).

Interestingly, in the end Jesus twists the tale. The lawyer had asked who is my neighbor, but Jesus concludes with an emphasis on who has been neighborly. The questioner is interested in who qualifies as neighbor. Jesus is interested in who among us is a good neighbor.

STRUGGLES WITH PREJUDICE

For the average Pharisee, loving your neighbor in this broad a definition would be out of the question. Their prejudices gave them permission to reduce their circle of involvement to people quite like themselves. And their prejudices were often supported by their self-constructed theology and traditions. Using these as an excuse got them off the hook for caring for the needs of those "other kind" of folk.

For instance, the Pharisees had nothing to do with tax collectors. These people were traitors of the worst kind. They had taken jobs with the occupying empire and collected exorbitant taxes. To add insult to injury, they added large assessments and pocketed them for themselves. The Pharisees stayed aloof lest they be seen as endorsing these horrid habits.

"Sinners" were in the same league. These were Jews who lived in total disregard of the law and openly and unashamedly flaunted their lifestyle. You don't have to wonder long why "sinners" did not make the list of those the Pharisees were responsible to love.

Samaritans were politically and religiously abhorrent to these gatekeepers of the true religion.

Women were off the screen as well, since they were viewed not only as chattel by the culture but also as sources of temptation and impurity. Ancient literature records that it was not uncommon for a Pharisee who saw a woman coming down the street to cross to the other side.

Other cultural prejudices were embraced as well. Shepherds, lepers, and beggars were added to the list of untouchables.

This is why the religious leaders were aghast that Jesus spent time with these groups. If Jesus' ministry proves anything, it dramatically demonstrates that no one is off His screen and that *prejudice* is not in His vocabulary. He touched the lepers. He healed blind beggars. He raised women to their rightful place of honor. He called Himself a shepherd. He ate with tax collectors and sinners. He even led revival meetings in Sychar, the capital of Samaria, after violating all the prejudicial codes by spending time with a Samaritan woman at the outskirts of town—an immoral woman at that.

Christ hates prejudice in any form. He detests racism, classism, and even religious snobbery. Why? Because they all cut across the very grain of who He is and what He came to do. Above and beyond everything else, He is a loving God who came to seek and save those who are lost. He is not, as some like to think, a God who loves only the best of us and hangs out with only the good guys.

Christ hates prejudice in any form because it cuts across the very grain of who He is and what He came to do.

Prejudice in any form kills our ability to love without limits and therefore strangles our capacity to love Christ. We cannot love someone we resent or someone we feel distanced from. And if we can't love our "neighbor," we can't love Christ. This is exactly what the apostle John meant when he wrote,

> If anyone says, "I love God," yet hates his brother, he is a liar. For anyone who does not love his brother, whom he has seen, cannot love God, whom he has not seen. And he has given us this command: Whoever loves God must also love his brother (1 John 4:20–21).

I can just hear the protests: "Who me? You've got to be kidding! I don't struggle with prejudice. I'm a new-millennium type of person. You're writing up the wrong tree. After all, didn't we all get over that in the sixties and seventies?"

Well, maybe. But I doubt it. In fact, we as a church may be more in the grip of prejudice today than ever before. We are angry about an awful lot of people, particularly in the light of the political and cultural revolutions we have experienced. We are angry about movies, music, prayer being taken out of the schools and condoms being put in. Opposition to gay liberation and abortion are justifiable concerns, yet they often turn our hearts against the sinners who perpetrate the sin.

What are your feelings toward the doctor who runs the abortion clinic in your town? Have you ever cared for him as a person and prayed that someone would lead him to the Savior? I wonder what our feelings are when we hear news of another abortion clinic practitioner being shot? Is there a sense of "Well, it serves him right"? Or do we weep for his soul?

People who are active in gay agendas often feel little but hate and judgment from our kind of people. And it's not that we shouldn't be discerning and clearly articulate our distaste for sin. However, Christ demonstrates the delicate, yet powerful, balance between knowing the weight of the sin without forgetting the worth of the sinner.

Not long ago, Matthew Shephard, a gay college student in Montana, was cruelly tortured and lynched in one of America's worst hate crimes. The news captured headlines and occupied hours of TV and radio talk shows. Outside the church where his funeral was being held, a minister carried a large placard that read, NO TEARS FOR QUEERS. While few of us would endorse such sub-Christian behavior, the pastor marching at Matthew Shephard's funeral became a media symbol of the attitudes of evangelical Christians. Our problem may be that instead of living compassionate lives, we have expressed our disdain in ways that give credence to that charge.

During the last two decades, many evangelical Christians have believed we could regain moral control of American culture through the political processes. We have threatened political parties who don't toe the line and berated politicians who don't bow to our wishes, calling them names and clogging their phone lines with well-orchestrated campaigns. We have used the church as a platform for political efforts and have often left people with the mistaken notion that becoming a Christian also means they must become right-wing Republicans.

Sadly, after literally millions of dollars and phenomenal amounts of time and energy, we are now realizing that we have failed to take America back through politics. In the wake of our realization that political companions have betrayed us, we angrily decry them as we pick up our political toys and leave. And all the while, no one in Washington gets the impression that we care for their souls. It seems clear that we were there to use them, not to love them.

Or think of walking through the mall and seeing a group of "alternative" teens approaching. As they get closer, you notice their arrogant swagger and their hair shaved on one side of their head and styled in red and orange spikes on the other. They have metal pierced into just about every conceivable place on their bodies, and their wrists are wrapped with leather bands sporting metal spikes.

What is your heart response? Do you pray as you walk by that someone will love them and lead them to Christ? Do you smile at them, hoping to let them know that someone our age really does care? Or does the revulsion in your soul win the day?

Our record with racial issues is not much better. While most of us are no longer blatantly racist, we continue to carry prejudicial attitudes in our hearts toward those of different colors and ethnic backgrounds. We look at some less-than-stellar records on economic initiative and marvel at the high crime and low morals of their communities. We then chalk it up to the idea that these really are not very good people after all. It's the old, "Why don't they get up off their fannies, get a job, and live decent lives like the rest of us do!" response. If the truth were known, there are many people in every cultural setting who tragically underperform—both personally and morally—regardless of skin color.

In fact, the minority elements in our society may be most like the man dying in the ditch in Jesus' story. Many of them are true victims. Many of the dynamics that created their degraded living conditions go all the way back to seeds that were planted when their ancestors were torn from their homes and brought to America as slaves. Slavery systematically dismantled the family structure of slaves on the plantation. It abusively downgraded their sense of worth and dignity. And to our shame, slavery was both tolerated and celebrated among many Christians, even to the point of creating a biblical justification for the inferiority of the black race.

After the liberation of the slaves, blacks were socially isolated and kept out of the mainstream of privilege and power. Mary McCleod Bethune is heralded today as one of the most outstanding African-American educators in history. She founded a college that still bears her name, and she is commemorated on a recent U.S. postage stamp. What most people don't know is that she came to Moody Bible Institute to become a missionary to her own people in Africa. Upon graduating from Moody, not one mission agency would accept her. So she couldn't go.

One of the worst subsidized housing developments in Chicago was planned to be a clustering of poor blacks. A federally funded highway was laid down as a barrier to keep them out of the ethnically powerful neighborhoods on the other side of the freeway. The "projects" that were built for them cost more than it would have cost to give each of them the money to buy their own home!

Our uncompassionate lecturing of what needy people ought to be doing is at best unproductive and at worst unloving.

> *Our uncompassionate lecturing of what needy*
> *people ought to be doing is at best unproductive*
> *and at worst unloving.*

These people didn't ask to be born into single-parent homes in the midst of drug- and gang-infested neighborhoods. Because of oppressive cultural systems that are sometimes intentionally put in place, there often is no way out for them. In our kind of "pull-yourself-up-by-your-bootstraps" Christianity, it is easy for us to say, "Buck up, be good, and get yourself out of there." Or simply blame them for the mess they are in. I suppose Jesus could have said, "Now we all know that the man from Jerusalem should not have traveled alone. Really, he should have known that was a horribly dangerous road. And why did he travel without a weapon? If he hadn't been wearing so much gold, those guys may not have been tempted to rob him. You know, don't you, that he always liked to flaunt his wealth. In a way it serves him right. . . ."

But for Jesus, the issue is never what the victim of sin should do to help himself. Rather, He says that those in need deserve redemptive love. This is exactly why Simon could not identify with the love feast at Jesus' feet nor understand the acceptance Jesus showed to a deplorable sinner. In Simon's mind, the woman didn't deserve forgiveness; she needed to stop doing what she was doing. If she would clean herself and her life up, there might be a chance of acceptance.

A friend of mine was recently called to the pulpit of a large, influential church in one of America's larger cities. It is a good church that has deep roots in the historical fabric of the city and has a passion to reach its city, as well as the world, for Christ. Part of the package for the senior pastor is a membership at the area's most prestigious golf club.

When my friend learned that the golf club excludes African-Americans, he graciously declined his membership. Then a member of the congregation came into his office holding a cube of wood with large nails protruding from it. Hoping to help the new pastor understand that there was good reason not to like minorities, he explained that after the assassination of Dr. Martin Luther King, the blacks in that city had thrown these into the streets for people to run over. In response, and at risk to himself and his future at the church, the pastor replied graciously, yet firmly, "You have to understand something: God hates racism, and so do I!"

Several months after arriving in town, my friend struck up a meaningful relationship with a black pastor. Together they are forging a slow but sure path that is breaking down walls that for generations have separated true followers of Christ in that city.

This pastor-friend is one of my heroes. His example encourages me to keep my heart clear of the prejudices that prevent me from loving my neighbors—all of them.

Developing a growing love relationship with our Lord requires that we acknowledge who our true neighbors are and then repent of the prejudice that has blocked our love for them and for Christ.

Biblical repentance demands that we change our minds about past thought patterns and then, as a result, change our behavior. While repentance is helped along by feelings of sorrow and remorse, it can be effected simply by acknowledging that something in our life is moving in the wrong direction and then turning our hearts and heads around.

*Loving Christ by loving our neighbors involves
thoughtful reflection and intentional planning.*

Loving Christ by loving our neighbors involves thoughtful reflection and intentional planning. The target is to develop a spirit of kindness to all who pass our way and mercy to the needy who surround our lives. The lawyer who questioned Jesus had it right. The neighborly one in the story was the one who showed mercy to the mugged man in the ditch. Jesus' response was that those who love their neighbors should go and do likewise.

It is time for reflection. To what kind of neighbors have you not felt much of a responsibility? Is it a matter of prejudice? Bitterness? Ignorance? Business? Apathy? Or have you just never thought of them as a neighbor worthy of your love? What plans can you make to extend merciful love in a neighborly way?

Your neighbor is the woman who sits through a green light in front of you, finishing her makeup while you are late to an appointment. It is the man in the "10-items-or-less" line at the grocery store who has seventeen items in his cart. And you know he has seventeen because you counted them! Your neighbor is the homeless man sitting in ragged clothes on the park bench.

From your "neighbors" in heavy traffic, to the neighbors next door, to the neighbors in the poorer sections of your town, to the most intimate "neighbors" who live under the same roof, Jesus made one thing crystal clear:

Loving Christ is about loving them.

CHAPTER NINE

THE ULTIMATE TESTIMONY

The Compelling Power of a Loving Community

The Chicago Lyric Opera's rendition of *Faust* profoundly portrays the tendency of the church to be less than merciful to sinners. In the story, Faust strikes a deal with the devil. The devil can have his soul in exchange for an extended life and the heart of the woman Faust has always desired. Both wishes are granted as the deal is struck. Faust finds and falls in love with the woman promised to him by the devil, and they have his desired affair.

Stirred by deep remorse, the young woman of Faust's dreams goes to church to seek forgiveness and cleansing from the guilt that weighs heavily on her soul. As she enters the church, the hooded monks in procession are chanting songs of judgment on sin and sinners. In a powerful symbol of gracelessness toward a troubled sinner, the producer of the Lyric Opera's version has the oversized crucifix hanging on one of the church pillars slowly turn upside down as the chanting continues. The message? The death of Christ would be of no avail to her in church.

Philip Yancey opens his book *What's So Amazing About Grace?* with a gripping story that should give all church folk pause. The story is told by a friend of his who works with the downtrodden in Chicago. It is not unlike the attitudes that filled the dining room at Simon's place.

> A prostitute came to me in wretched straits, homeless, sick, unable to buy food for her two-year-old daughter. Through sobs and tears, she told me that she had been renting out her daughter—two years old!—to men interested in kinky sex. She made more renting out her daughter for an hour than she could earn on her own in a whole night. She had to do it, she said, to support her own drug habit. I could hardly bear hearing her sordid story. For one thing, it made me legally liable—I'm required to report cases of child abuse. I had no idea what to say to this woman.
>
> At last I asked if she had ever thought of going to a church for help. I will never forget the look of pure, naive shock that crossed her face. "Church?" she said. "Why would I ever go there? I was already feeling terrible about myself. They'd just make me feel worse."[1]

Yancey then observes, "What struck me about my friend's story is that women much like this prostitute fled toward Jesus, not away from him. . . . Evidently the down-and-out, who flocked to Jesus when he lived on earth, no longer feel welcome among his followers." In Jesus' day people like this woman approached Christ and found refuge, comfort, and forgiveness. Has the church lost the heart of Christ?

Stories like this shock our grace-protected sensitivities. Yet, even as we recoil from the power of depravity to plunge people to such dark depths, we should be equally struck with this woman's words about the church. Sadly, her condemning perspective cannot be written off as the distorted point of view of a down-and-out vagrant. If we look candidly at our churches, we would find too few whose testimony in the community resounds as a place where love prevails, a place known for people who care about each other and about the most despairing in their community.

If my assessment is true, then we have failed in our most fundamental mission. At the close of His ministry, Jesus turned to His disciples and cast His vision for the church. He did it in the form of a command—a command that has become the illusive dream of Christ's work in our world. And while most of us could readily recite His words from memory, it remains an enigma why it seems so difficult to live them out. Jesus said,

> "A new command I give you: Love one another. As I have loved you, so you must love one another. By this all men will know that you are my disciples, if you love one another" (John 13:34–35).

To fulfill Christ's mandate, love must drive and define the work and reputation of the church. Yet, of all the impressions that the world has of the church, the least is that we love each other with a compassion that speaks to their loveless and hurting lives.

REACHING NEEDS THROUGH CHURCH

This coldness was not the reputation of followers of Christ in the early days of the church. Ostracized and persecuted, the first-century Christians were forced to live out this command in a dynamic way. They shared their goods, defended one another in the face of hostile threats, welcomed anyone who would bow the knee to the Master of their souls, and forgave even the worst of sinners and enemies.

Of all the impressions that the world has of the church, the least is that we love each other with a compassion that speaks to their loveless and hurting lives.

Why? Because they loved Christ and sought to reflect the love that He not only commanded, but demonstrated, on the cross. It was the power of this love that caught the attention of the pagan world in which they lived. In fact, secular sources of that day mention that it was often said about those early followers, "See how they love one another."

Historian Will Durant, who is often contemptuous or amused by Christianity, writes of the rise of the church in the days of Caesar. Durant draws this relevant and timely observation:

> All in all, no more attractive religion has ever been presented to mankind. It offered itself without restrictions to all individuals, classes, and nations; it was not limited to one people, like Judaism, nor to the free-men of one state, like the official cults of Greece and Rome. By making all men heirs of Christ's victory over death, Christianity announced the basic equality of men, and made transiently trivial all differences of earthly degree. To the miserable, maimed, bereaved, disheartened, and humiliated it brought the new virtue of compassion, and an ennobling dignity; it gave them the inspiring figure, story, and ethic of Christ; it brightened their lives with the hope of the coming Kingdom, and of endless happiness beyond the grave. To even the greatest sinners it promised forgiveness, and their full acceptance into the community of the saved. To minds harassed with the insoluble problems of origin and destiny, evil and suffering, it brought a system of divinely revealed doctrine in which the simplest soul could find mental rest. To men and women imprisoned in the prose of poverty and toil it brought the poetry of the sacraments. . . .
>
> Into the moral vacuum of a dying paganism, into the coldness of Stoicism and the corruption of Epicureanism, into a world sick of brutality, cruelty, oppression, and sexual chaos, into a pacified empire that seemed no longer to need the masculine virtues of the gods of war, it brought a new morality of brotherhood, kindliness, decency, and peace. So molded to men's wants, the new faith spread with fluid readiness. Nearly every convert, with the ardor of a revolutionary, made himself an office of propaganda.[2]

Unlike those early followers, most of us did not come to church because we needed the healing touch of love. We go to church because it is where we grew up or because we feel it is the right thing to do. It provides a niche where we can belong and, in a sense, pay our religious dues. We do church because we like the music, the preacher, the youth program, or the atmosphere. We meet our friends and build our social networking there. It is a place where we can teach and lead and occupy positions of influence and power. In short, it is a place where we often go to satisfy ourselves without much thought at all to loving others who are there. In fact, if we are not satisfied with what is going on at church, we get grumpy about it, complain, find another church, or just quit attending altogether.

Of course, the big problem in many churches today is that people have varied tastes in music. I remember thinking, when I left the pastorate to serve at Moody, that at least I wouldn't have to worry about the music problem anymore. In my dreams! Moody owns and operates twenty-eight radio stations across the United States, on which we play music sixty percent of the time. Our challenge is to minister to a broad section of tastes and to cultivate a new generation of young people who will be encouraged in their faith, perhaps attend Moody, and partner with our work for Christ in the years ahead. While the stations regularly play segments that target an older listening group, much of the music that is aired is geared toward younger tastes. As a result, some music doesn't meet the expectations of older listeners.

The most hostile mail I have received is about music. The letters have included long explanations of why letting music "standards" down is the first step to heresy and doctrinal drift. Some have made angry threats to stop sending donations and to take Moody out of their wills. While we are reaching far more people today than ever through radio, the only thing that seems to matter to some people is that their own needs should be met.

But not everyone sees ministries through the narrow scope of "what is best for me." Sometime ago I received a letter from an eighty-four-year-old woman who made it clear that she did not like most of the music we play on the Moody radio stations. But she explained that when she was a teenager, someone ministered to her at her level, and she accepted Christ as her Savior. She said that if young people are being reached for Christ through the music, then she was rejoicing and would encourage us to stay at it. What a refreshing and rare perspective!

Creating an atmosphere of love among believers is a tough challenge. Churches that take steps to reach out to those in need often come under fire. Other Christians accuse them of simply pandering to a consumer mentality. Critics sanctimoniously insist that it is the church's singular task to preach the Word and let the impact of the spoken truth take care of all needs. And while the Word must always be paramount, they talk as though there is no need for sermonic words about love to become incarnate in action.

On occasion churches seem more interested in budgets and buildings than in programs designed to reach people in need. Perhaps this is due in part to the fact that we don't foster an environment where needs are known. We wear our best faces to church and are rarely willing to be vulnerable enough to let our true needs show. So there is no "show-and-tell" about what needs to be fixed way down inside. We fear that self-revelation may be misunderstood and that we may become marginalized or gossiped about. We tend to live by an unspoken "don't ask, don't tell" policy. The problem is, when everything appears okay with everyone, there is not much opportunity to love or to give to others in need.

If we love Christ, we must become a community of belief whose actions are characterized by the quality of Christ's love for us.

But if we love Christ, then we must turn away from self-focused Christianity. We must become a community of belief whose actions are characterized by the quality of Christ's love for us. When that happens, the impact becomes immeasurable.

Having spoken about our failure to love one another, I must admit that there are many churches today that are taking the charge seriously.

Their effectiveness for Christ is a living testimony to the importance of His command.

A church in the suburbs of Chicago runs a program geared to changing the oil, greasing, and fixing problems of broken-down cars. At first glance a program like that at church might appear to be a waste of time—it's not "spiritual." But consider this: The church realized that many in the congregation are single moms who struggle to make ends meet and are unable to deal with car problems on their own. In fact, often they are victimized by unscrupulous mechanics. Since there are mechanics in the congregation, they decided to open shop every Monday night to fix and maintain cars. The moms have been genuinely loved and cared for. You can imagine the response of one's unsaved friends and family when she tells them who maintains her car!

A church on the south side of Chicago is composed of people who left the comfort of their affluent suburban lifestyle and moved into the neighborhood where the church was being planted. They plan to develop a program that would have homeless people move in with member families. Does that sound risky? It is. But then sometimes true love is risky. It was for Jesus. This new church has started with an agenda to love. May it never lose its passion!

Because of their outspoken opposition to unrighteousness, Armitage Baptist Church was targeted by groups of radical abortion and gay activists to embarrass and defame the church in the community. In the weeks before a scheduled demonstration, the planners canvassed the residents of the area, inviting them to join in the protest and swell the ranks. Some communities surrounding a church might respond in large numbers. But on the night of the march, not one neighbor could be found, and the number of protesters proved to be embarrassingly small.

I asked the pastor why no neighbors came. He explained that through the years Armitage Baptist has intentionally reached out to its community with programs that meet real needs. When the Chicago schoolteachers went on strike for several weeks at the beginning of one school year, teachers in the congregation held school at the church for neighborhood children. The pastor told me that their community knows that the church cares for them and that no one would want to join a protest like the one being staged that night.

At a church in Dallas, one of its young men got into trouble with the law. Church officials went to the judge and asked him to release the accused into the care of a church elder. They presented to the judge a well-designed program of accountability and rehabilitation. The judge accepted the proposal and turned the boy over to the custody of the church. At the end of the process, the judge dismissed the charges as a result of the church's redemptive impact on the young man's life. A few weeks later, the judge called the church. You guessed it: He wondered whether the church would be willing to take any other juvenile offenders into their care. The church did, and to this day it has a program that has caught the attention of a judicial system that is confronted with overcrowded dockets and full-to-capacity jails.

Pastor Ed Dobson of Calvary Church in Grand Rapids, Michigan, realized that there were many marginalized people in his church who rarely felt comfortable with traditional Sunday services. To lovingly reach these "outsiders" who were brothers and sisters in Christ, he designed a Saturday evening service that ministered to them in their cultural and heart language. The service exploded in size and has proved to be a drawing card not only for followers of Christ but for nonbelievers as well. Dobson's loving leadership rubbed off on those who attended, and as a result his church has had an impact for Christ among the gay community and many others who had never been reached by churches before.

There is no telling what churches full of Christ-lovers can do when they commit themselves to show a Christlike love to alienated and empty lives that surround them. Think what it would mean to people looking for love if they knew they could find it among the followers of Christ. The church and other groups of committed Christians would be like magnets to draw loveless lives to Christ. Moreover, it would not be just the unloved who would be curiously impressed. Everyone is warmed by loving environments. Loving followers of Christ reflect the glory of their Lord and become a drawing card, in the same way that Jesus' love drew the masses to His side.

> *There is no telling what churches full of Christ-*
> *lovers can do when they commit themselves to show*
> *a Christlike love to alienated and empty lives that*
> *surround them.*

What Jesus is saying is that we who belong to Him and who have been loved by Him have a moral obligation—no, a moral *privilege*—to take all His love that we have experienced and turn it outward in the direction of one another. And the decision to love others as He has loved us starts, not as a corporate resolve, but with each of us individually. Loving is not sitting around to see whether people are going to get on board. Whether anyone else does or not, our love for Christ calls us to reach out to the needs and nurture of people regardless of the crowd or the cost. Starting where it may be the toughest, with our brothers and sisters, it then creates a compelling draw.

TAKING LOVE PERSONALLY

What does it take to love "one another," our brothers and sisters in Christ? I am reminded of the ditty that goes

> To dwell above with saints we loved,
> O that will be glory.
> But to dwell below with saints we know—
> Well, that's a different story.

The key to love is found in the roots of Christ's command. When He said this was a *new* command, He meant new in quality, not in time. It is like Proctor and Gamble saying that you can buy "new and improved TIDE." It is not a new product; it is an improvement on the old.

There is a sequence here that would have struck a responsive cord in the disciples' minds. In the previous chapter we looked at the two "great" commands: Love God with the totality of your being, and love your neighbor as you love yourself. When Jesus tells His disciples to love one another as He has loved them, the similarity to the great commands is apparent. But the new command has both a new focus and a higher standard.

The new focus is not on our neighbors but on our fellow followers as the object of our love. This does not negate our responsibility to neighbors; it simply calls us to make loving those in God's family a visible priority. No doubt Christ knows that if we can love cantankerous Christians, loving our neighbor will be a snap.

The new standard is not based on how we love ourselves but on how Christ has loved us. If we are to love others as Christ loved us, then we have a wonderful template to measure our love by. For three intensive years the disciples watched and experienced the love of Christ showered on their lives. Even a quick study of His loving ways reveals some important patterns.

Jesus loved the disciples regardless of their temperament problems. This group had some serious quirks—Peter, for example. Have you ever been around someone who is inherently verbal? Someone who constantly has an answer and is always first to voice a commitment to the next cause? Peter is always in the forefront of everyone's attention. He is the first guy out of the boat. He's walking on the water. He's telling Jesus that he will never betray Him. He's cutting off the soldier's ear in the garden. You would really like to tell Peter to chill out!

Andrew is another interesting study. Although he is cast in the positive light of bringing many to Jesus, he appears to be hardly verbal at all. The only time Andrew is recorded as saying anything is the occasion of the feeding of the five thousand. Looking for food to feed the gathered crowd, Andrew finds a boy who has brown-bagged it to the revival service. The boy's lunch consists of five loaves and two fish. So Andrew brings the child to Jesus and says, "But what are these among so many?" All day long Andrew has been watching Jesus heal the sick and make the blind to see, but at this moment there is no thought that Jesus may want to do a miracle with the boy's lunch. (I feel like telling Andrew that if he is going to say something to be recorded in Scripture, then at least he should make it meaningful.)

Living with John is like living with a split personality. He is the one who writes about love more than any other New Testament author. Yet his nickname is "Son of Thunder," which indicates that he had an explosive disposition. At one point he asked Jesus to call down lightning on His enemies. You want to tell a guy like John to get his act together: Either be loving or vindictive, but not both.

And of course we can't fail to mention Thomas, the skeptic. If you ever want to have a "fun-filled" evening, invite every cynic and skeptic you know to your party. They will all sit around and say, "Oh yeah? Prove it. . . . I told you so." Do you think Jesus liked Thomas's doubting? The book of Hebrews says that "without faith it is impossible to please God" (Heb. 11:6).

> *Don't wait to* like *your brothers and sisters in Christ before you* love *them.*

I doubt that Jesus liked these or any other examples of antisocial behavior exhibited among His followers, but He loved them just the same. This proves a very important point: Don't wait to *like* your brothers and sisters in Christ before you *love* them. Christlike love transcends what you like or don't like and goes right to the needs of the one you love. Loving people you like is easy. The challenge is to love one another even when someone rubs you the wrong way.

Jesus also loved His disciples across social and economic barriers. Among any group of followers we can usually find a variety of backgrounds and economic standing. This means that pulling into the church parking lot is going to be a relatively intimidating experience, especially if you see quite a few Lexuses or BMWs and you're driving a beat-up old Chevy. If you happen to park next to the family in the big black Mercedes, are you going to greet them sincerely and let them know that cars don't make a bit of difference among God's people? Or, as you smile and wave, are you saying under your breath, "If he loved the Lord, he'd never drive a car like that. He'd give all his money to missions." Or, if this is the day that you have brought your neighbors to church in your BMW, do you privately wish the family of eight pouring out of the rusted minivan would have parked somewhere out of sight? We have trouble with the differences in how we dress, the color of our skin, the size of our bank accounts, and just about anything that produces class and culture differences.

The disciples come from dramatically different backgrounds. James, John, Peter, and Andrew are fisherman. These are the tough guys who probably still have the smell of fish on their robes. They are the truck drivers of their day. Then you've got a sophisticated businessman, Matthew, who collects exorbitant taxes and is hated for his dishonesty and allegiance to Rome. And since we're considering the social, economic, class mix of the disciples, don't forget to include Simon the Zealot. He was a member of the resistance force committed to overthrowing the Roman oppressors. Yet, across all of these otherwise divisive barriers Jesus loves them all, equally, without prejudice or preference.

Jesus loves them with His time, talent, and energy. After a busy day of ministry, Jesus gets in a boat and tells the disciples to take Him to the other side of the lake. Exhausted, He goes down into the hold of the ship and falls fast asleep just as a storm begins to blow, threatening the lives of all concerned.

But Jesus is rudely awakened by His frantic disciples. They think they are going to die, and Jesus is their last chance to survive. I doubt that they tiptoed in and gently whispered to their Lord. Be assured that they came yelling, "Lord, Lord, we're dying! Wake up!" If I were Jesus, I would have said, "Where is your faith? Do you think the kingdom is going down to Davy Jones's locker in this lake? Now let Me go back to sleep."

The Lord didn't do that. In the depth of their trauma, He got up one more time to love them with His time, talents, and energy. He stood up and spoke to the storm, and it was stilled. Only then did He say, "Let me tell you about faith." Loving one another sometimes means that we need to give our energy and talents even when we'd rather be in bed.

Jesus loved them by laying down His life. We know that the ultimate way Jesus loved both the disciples and us was by dying on the cross. The apostle John writes, "This is how we know what love is: Jesus Christ laid down his life for us. And we ought to lay down our lives for our brothers" (1 John 3:16). This isn't something we do merely by one dramatic act of martyrdom. When we follow Christ's example of love, we live each day sacrificially. John goes on to say, "Dear children, let us not love with words or tongue but with actions and in truth" (v. 18). John gives one practical example how to do this: "If anyone has material possessions and sees his brother in need but has no pity on him, how can the love of God be in him?" (v. 17). Christlike love first involves seeing people's needs and then meeting them in tangible, sacrificial ways.

> *Love is our validating testimony to a watching*
> *world that we are His followers.*

Jesus says that if we learn to love each other like this, our love will be the living proof that we belong to Him. Love is our validating testimony to a watching world that we are His followers. The poor prostitute who sold her two-year-old daughter should have found the church a place of redeeming love instead of self-righteous condemnation. Many of us have grown up in church environments where the way to show you're a Christian is by not drinking, dancing, smoking, or running around with those who do. But Christ says the true sign that shows we are His followers is that we love each other in the very same way He loved us.

In my book *Following Christ* I mentioned that one of my favorite churches is the Gospel House, which is south of Cleveland. It was started by two men who were evangelists to prisoners. As they led prisoners to the Lord, they encouraged them to go to church when their sentences were up and they were out of jail. Unfortunately, the churches recommended to the new believers did not reach out to these ex-cons, and they were made to feel quite unwelcome. Not knowing what to do, someone suggested that the evangelists start their own church for these newly redeemed and released prisoners. So they did.

The church is a fascinating place. It has grown dramatically and is now full of not only rejoicing former prisoners but also ex-prostitutes, business executives, single parents, black folk, and Latino folk. It's like heaven—some from every tribe and nation are there. But what touches me most is the sense of love one feels in that church.

The church has a wonderful ritual, and if I ever return to the pastorate, it is something I would like to institute. At a particular point in their worship service, they invite anyone with a need to come and kneel at the front of the church. As the singing continues, hurting and burdened people stream forward and kneel while men and women from the congregation come and place their hands on their shoulders, kneel next to them, and pray with them. It is a liturgy of love as tears flow and burdens are shared at the feet of the Savior in prayer.

The last time I was there, I noticed a disabled woman in the front row of the choir. Her body was gnarled with seemingly every joint going the wrong way. Next to her was a woman who was obviously blind; she had memorized the choir number. Both women lifted their faces to God in unrestrained praise. I thanked the pastor after the service for graphically displaying the love of Christ in the front row of the choir. The unspoken message was loaded with symbols of the limitless love of Christ.

As important as it is to love Christ by loving one another, Scripture affirms that there is one focus of love that profoundly touches the heart of Christ.

CHAPTER TEN

STREET LOVE

Giving the Disadvantaged the Advantage of His Love

Michael Brock is a wealthy, upwardly mobile lawyer in a posh and sophisticated law firm in Washington, D.C. He is the fictitious hero of John Grisham's novel *Street Lawyer,* and his attitude toward the disadvantaged entails a script that could be written about many of us.

> The man with the rubber boots stepped into the elevator behind me, but I didn't see him at first. I smelled him though—the pungent odor of smoke and cheap wine and life on the street without soap. We were alone as we moved upward, and when I finally glanced over I saw the boots, black and dirty and much too large. A frayed and tattered trench coat fell to his knees. Under it layers of foul clothing bunched around his mid-section, so that he appeared stocky, almost fat. . . . He was black and aging. . . . He didn't belong. It was not his building, not his elevator, not a place he could afford. . . . Just another street bum in from the cold. . . . We had security guards to deal with the riffraff.[1]

The "street bum," as Brock labels him, gets off the elevator as well and soon has Mr. Brock and seven of his colleagues lined up at gunpoint in the lavishly outfitted walnut-wrapped boardroom of the firm. The once proud and powerful eight are paralyzed with fear as hostages. In time the homeless man, who wants to be called "Mister," asks each of them how much money they made in the previous year. Massive six-figure amounts roll from their tongues. Mister then asks how much they have given to the poor and the homeless. Their feeble responses indict each one as one by one they recite their embarrassing and rather token nod of the checkbook to the less fortunate.

With a savvy that belies his smelly, impoverished condition, Mister asks Brock who fills out the IRS forms for the lawyers in the firm. Brock replies that the accountants in the accounting department tend to the tax returns. Mister demands that the accountants be delivered to the boardroom. He then has Brock read off the total income for each of the trembling attorneys and then the paltry amounts of their charitable giving and to whom the money had been distributed.

I was hooked on the book, but not just by the suspense of the opening chapters. I was reading this Grisham tale as I sat on a comfortable chaise longue at the edge of a beautiful pool overlooking the brilliant blue waters of the ocean. As the warmth of the sun convinced me that this is the way life should be lived, the Holy Spirit was using a novel to convict and probe deeply my own heart and attitudes.

I found myself wondering, if the homeless man had been Christ and I had been Brock, whether my tax return would have satisfied Christ that I love Him by loving the disadvantaged? Or would the tax return be a source of embarrassment and shame?

For emerging Christ-lovers this is a pivotal question. Of all the ways that He explains we can touch Him with our love, helping the helpless is by far the most neglected. Most of us live in comfortable environments well insulated from the needs of the despairing. From our privileged vantage point it becomes easy to write off the needs of the less fortunate. Too often we see them as irresponsible or dangerous. I have to admit that for years this kind of thinking governed my perspective. Then we moved to Chicago and were confronted with the

reality that many of the disadvantaged in American society are true victims and have very little hope on their own to rescue themselves.
Whether we like to think it or not, many are buried under the weight
of economic and social structures that place them in the bondage of
despair. I often wonder what it was that justified my being born into
the privilege of a God-fearing, middle-class home where opportunities
for advancement were abundant while so many, through no choice of
their own, are born into the dismal poverty of a fatherless life on the
wrong side of town—the side of town where financial security is best
achieved by networking with the local drug dealers and where safety,
security, and social status are found most readily in the gang structure.

We cannot ignore the fact that Christ is deeply interested in what
we do to aid the disadvantaged. And, in fact, that He sees our activity
on this front as a major statement of the authenticity of our love for Him.

> "When the Son of Man comes in his glory, and all the angels
> with him, he will sit on his throne in heavenly glory. All the
> nations will be gathered before him, and he will separate the
> people one from another as a shepherd separates the sheep
> from the goats. He will put the sheep on his right and the
> goats on his left.
>
> "Then the King will say to those on his right, 'Come,
> you who are blessed by my Father; take your inheritance,
> the kingdom prepared for you since the creation of the
> world. For I was hungry and you gave me something to eat,
> I was thirsty and you gave me something to drink, I was a
> stranger and you invited me in, I needed clothes and you
> clothed me, I was sick and you looked after me, I was in
> prison and you came to visit me.'
>
> "Then the righteous will answer him, 'Lord, when
> did we see you hungry and feed you, or thirsty and give you
> something to drink? When did we see you a stranger and
> invite you in, or needing clothes and clothe you? When did
> we see you sick or in prison and go to visit you?'

"The King will reply, 'I tell you the truth, whatever you did for one of the least of these brothers of mine, you did for me'" (Matt. 25:31–40).

Craig Phillips is an heir to the Wrigley fortune and was well on his way to wealth and prominence in his own right until he was confronted with loving Christ by reaching out to the disadvantaged. Since that encounter he has founded two churches, and at the age of eighty-four he volunteers at the Wayside Cross Mission in Aurora, Illinois.

I was working in the Loop as a young 27-year-old and had been gifted with a fine position in one of the Corporate 500 companies. I was walking from the suburban train station coming in from the North shore into the Loop. I walked by the "L" as I would do many mornings, and I'd see people lying in there. One morning I was on the way to my beautiful corporate office with my nice clothes, and my nice tie on and my expensive shoes, and I walked by this alley and saw this broken man lying underneath an elevator where the hot air was coming out for some warmth. Chicago's interesting because on one side is the very elite and right behind it is the very devastating. I walked by, but I couldn't go any further. I turned around and walked back in the alley. I went up to that man and asked, "Is that you, Jesus?" I knew it wasn't Jesus, but I knew that that is where Jesus would be. I said, "Lord, am I on the wrong track looking after material things?" And he said, "Yes, Craig, you are. I told you that a long time ago." And so that's when I changed my goal and went back to what God had touched me as a little boy and said, "Look at the heart, don't look at the outside. God will always reward you."

Since then my life has been a joy because there are so many broken things in life that Jesus can fix. When you let Him do it, you share in that joy. It's greater than any riches you could ever have. It's greater than any material thing. One word with somebody has the power to pick him up and show him Jesus, and let him know that Jesus loves him. No amount of materialism can ever replace that. That lasts for eternity. That's where your treasure is. That's where your heart will be. And no one can take it from you. You can never lose that.

I've always said that if you gain the world, you lose your soul. But if you gain your soul, you don't mind losing the world. People around us are dying. They are waiting. The one in the penthouse, the corporate office and the one in the alley. They need to know just one thing. He died for them and He loves them. He's not willing that any should perish. He's waiting for them. He's knocking at the door. He's real. He's here. He's in Chicago. He's in your house. He's on your street. He's in your life, and He desires to be in everyone's life. How many times has He wept over Jerusalem, and I think how many times He's weeping over this area, this city of ours, waiting for each one of us to share the Good News. He'll give you that joy when you do. He'll give you that peace. He said it's worth it all. It's worth it all.[2]

After a session in which I had taught a group of ministry leaders about the importance of loving Christ through loving the poor and oppressed, one of the participants who is involved in "street ministry" approached me. He said, "I have trouble getting a grip on loving Christ because I can't see Him or be with Him. But I have found that I can see Jesus in people I minister to. When I love them, I know that I am loving Him. It is their presence in my life that brings me close to Him."

"FOR I SHALL COME . . ."

Loving Christ by loving the disadvantaged is a truth that has gripped sincere Christ-lovers for centuries.

Leo Tolstoy, the author of the great classic *War and Peace,* wrote many short stories, including a lesser-known one entitled "Where Love Is, God Is."[3] The story is about a Russian shoemaker, Martin Avdéitch, who has lived a very difficult and disappointing life. His wife died early on, and all his children died in infancy or early youth. He has become a bitter man and reproaches God, praying that he, too, might die. But in the depths of his bitterness an old man shows Martin the forgiveness of God, and his life is radically transformed. As Tolstoy unfolds this story, Martin the shoemaker is reading the account of our hero, the sinful woman of Luke 7, as she comes to Simon's house. Martin notes Simon's less than cordial treatment of Christ. Convicted, Martin the shoemaker says,

> "He must have been like me, that Pharisee. He too thought only of himself—how to get a cup of tea, how to keep warm and comfortable; never a thought of his guest. He took care of himself, but for his guest he cared nothing at all. Yet who was the guest? The Lord himself! If he came to me, should I behave like that?'
>
> Then Martin laid his head upon both his arms and, before he was aware of it, he fell asleep.
>
> "Martin!" he suddenly heard a voice, as if someone had breathed the word above his ear.
>
> He started from his sleep. "Who's there?" he asked.
>
> He turned around and looked at the door; no one was there. He called again. Then he heard quite distinctly: "Martin, Martin! Look out into the street tomorrow, for I shall come." . . .
>
> Next morning he rose before daylight, and after saying his prayers he lit the fire and prepared his cabbage soup and buckwheat porridge. Then he lit the samovár, put on his apron, and sat down by the window to his work. As he sat working, Martin thought over what had happened the night before. At times it seemed to him like a dream, and at times he thought that he had really heard the voice. "Such things have happened before now," thought he.
>
> So he sat by the window, looking out into the street more than he worked, and whenever any one passed in unfamiliar boots he would stoop and look up, so as to see not

the feet only but the face of the passer-by as well. A house-porter passed in new felt boots; then a water-carrier. Presently an old soldier of Nicholas' reign came near the window, spade in hand. Martin knew him by his boots, which were shabby old felt ones, galoshed with leather. The old man was called Stepánitch; a neighboring tradesman kept him in his house for charity, and his duty was to help the house-porter. He began to clear away the snow before Martin's window. Martin glanced at him and then went on with his work.

"I must be growing crazy with age," said Martin, laughing at his fancy. "Stepánitch comes to clear away the snow, and I must needs imagine it's Christ coming to visit me. Old dotard that I am!"

Yet after he had made a dozen stitches, he felt drawn to look out of the window again. He saw that Stepánitch had leaned his spade against the wall, and was either resting himself or trying to get warm. The man was old and broken down, and had evidently not enough strength even to clear away the snow. . . .

Martin beckoned to him to come in and went himself to open the door.

"Come in," he said, "and warm yourself a bit. I'm sure you must be cold."

"May God bless you!" Stepánitch answered. "My bones do ache to be sure." He came in, first shaking off the snow, and lest he should leave marks on the floor, he began wiping his feet; but as he did so he tottered and nearly fell.

"Don't trouble to wipe your feet," said Martin. "I'll wipe up the floor—it's all in the day's work. Come, friend, sit down and have some tea."

Filling two tumblers, he passed one to his visitor, and pouring his own out into the saucer, began to blow on it.

Stepánitch emptied his glass, and, turning it upside down, put the remains of his piece of sugar on the top. He began to express his thanks, but it was plain that he would be glad of some more.

"Have another glass," said Martin, refilling the visitor's tumbler and his own. But while he drank his tea, Martin kept looking out into the street.

"Are you expecting anyone?" asked the visitor.

"Am I expecting any one? Well, now, I'm ashamed to tell you. It isn't that I really expect any one; but I heard something last night which I can't get out of my mind Whether it was a vision, or only a fancy, I can't tell. You see, friend, last night I was reading the Gospel, about Christ the Lord, how he suffered, and how he walked on earth. You have heard tell of it, I dare say."

"I have heard tell of it," answered Stepánitch, "but I'm an ignorant man and not able to read."

"Well, you see, I was reading of how he walked on earth. I came to that part, you know, where he went to a Pharisee who did not receive him well. Well, friend, as I read about it, I thought now that man did not receive Christ the Lord with proper honor. Suppose such a thing could happen to such a man as myself, I thought, what would I not do to receive him! But that man gave him no reception at all. Well, friend, as I was thinking of this, I began to doze, and as I dozed I heard some one call me by name. I got up, and thought I heard some one whispering, 'Expect me; I will come to-morrow.' This happened twice over. And to tell you the truth, it sank so into my mind that, though I am ashamed of it myself, I keep on expecting him, the dear Lord!"

Stepánitch shook his head in silence, finished his tumbler, and laid it on its side; but Martin stood it up again and refilled it for him.

"Here drink another glass, bless you! And I was thinking too, how he walked on earth and despised no one, but went mostly among common folk. He went with plain people, and chose his disciples from among the likes of us, from workmen like us, sinners that we are. 'He who raises himself,' he said, 'shall be humbled and he who humbles himself shall be raised.' 'You call me Lord,' he said, 'and I will wash your feet.' 'He who would be first,' he said, 'let him be the servant of all; because,' he said, 'blessed are the poor, the humble, the meek, and the merciful.'"

Stepánitch forgot his tea. He was an old man easily moved to tears, and as he sat and listened, the tears ran down his cheeks. . . .

"Thank you, Martin Avdéitch," he said, "you have given me food and comfort both for soul and body." . . .

Stepánitch went away; and Martin poured out the last of the tea and drank it up. Then he put away the tea things and sat down to his work, stitching the back seam of a boot. And as he stitched, he kept looking out of the window, waiting for Christ, and thinking about him and his doings. And his head was full of Christ's sayings.

As Martin worked, two soldiers went by, one in government boots and the other in his own. Then the master of a neighboring house, in shining galoshes, passed the house. Then a baker carrying a basket.

Then a woman came up in worsted stockings and peasant-made shoes. She passed the window, but stopped by the wall. Martin glanced up at her through the window and saw that she was a stranger, poorly dressed, and with a baby in her arms. . . . The woman had only summer clothes on, and even they were shabby and worn. Through the window Martin heard the baby crying, and the woman trying to soothe it, but unable to do so. Martin rose and going out of the door and up the steps he called to her. . . .

"There, sit down, my dear, near the stove. Warm yourself. And feed the baby."

"Haven't any milk. I have eaten nothing myself since early morning," said the woman. . . .

Martin shook his head. He brought out a basin and some bread. Then he opened the oven door and poured some cabbage soup into the basin. . . .

"Haven't you any warmer clothing?" he asked.

"How could I get warm clothing?" said she. "Why, I pawned my last shawl for sixpence yesterday.". . . .

Martin looked among some things that were hanging on the wall and brought back an old cloak.

"Here," he said, "though it's a worn-out old thing, it will do to wrap him up in."

The woman looked at the cloak, then at the old man, and taking it, burst into tears. . . .

"The Lord bless you, friend. Surely Christ must have sent me to your window, else the child would have frozen. It was mild when I started, but now see how cold it has turned. Surely it must have been Christ who made you look out of your window and take pity on me, poor wretch!"

Martin smiled and said; "It is quite true; it was he made me do it. It was no mere chance made me look out.". . .

"Take this for Christ's sake," said Martin, and gave her sixpence to get her shawl out of pawn. The woman crossed herself, and Martin did the same, and then he saw her out. . . .

After the woman had gone, Martin . . . sat and worked, but did not forget the window, and every time a shadow fell on it he looked up at once to see who was passing. People he knew and strangers passed by, but no one remarkable. . . .

The day wore on, and soon it began to grow dark.

"Seems it's time to light up," thought he. So he trimmed his lamp, hung it up, and sat down again to work. He finished off one boot and, turning it about, examined it. It was all right. Then he gathered his tools together, swept up the cuttings, put away the bristles and the thread and the awls, and, taking down the lamp, placed it on the table. Then he took the Gospels from the shelf. He meant to open them at the place he had marked the day before with a bit of morocco, but the book opened at another place. As Martin opened it, his yesterday's dream came back to his mind, and no sooner had he thought of it than he seemed to hear footsteps, as though someone were moving behind him. Martin turned around, and it seemed to him as if people were standing in the dark corner, but he could not make out who they were. And a voice whispered in his ear: "Martin, Martin, don't you know me?"

"Who is it?" muttered Martin.

"It is I," said the voice. And out of the dark corner stepped Stepánitch, who smiled and, vanishing like a cloud, was seen no more.

"It is I," said the voice again. And out of the darkness stepped the woman with the baby in her arms, and the woman smiled and the baby laughed, and they too vanished. . . .

And Martin's soul grew glad. He crossed himself, put on his spectacles, and began reading the Gospel just where it had opened; and at the top of the page he read,

"I was an hungred, and ye gave me meat: I was thirsty, and ye gave me drink: I was a stranger, and ye took me in."

And at the bottom of the page he read,

"Inasmuch as ye did it unto one of these my brethren even these least, ye did it unto me" (Matt. xxv).

And Martin understood that his dream had come true; and that the Savior had really come to him that day, and he had welcomed him.

Martin Avdéitch had come to understand what all of us need to understand. The best way to distance oneself from Simon is to entertain the needs of the truly needy and in that way know the joy of expressing our love to Christ.

ALL THE RIGHT THINGS

My father is now eighty-nine years old. He is a godly man who along with my mother has faithfully served the Lord for decades. Without fail, whenever my dad would write to me, at the bottom of the letter he always put his "life verse"—Isaiah 58:10–11. I do not know whether I would be struck with these verses now if I hadn't been, since a young boy, acquainted with them through my dad's life and his recurring notations.

The passage is a powerful statement of what God thinks about the oppressed and disadvantaged. In the broader context, the Israelites are complaining about the fact that they don't seem to feel very connected to God even though, in their minds, they are doing all the right things. They recite a long list of their faithful acts of service, including what we would today call daily devotions and fasting.

God replies to their self-righteous complaint by saying that the reason for feeling out of touch is that they are *not* doing the things He desires. God says,

> "Is not this the kind of fasting I have chosen:
> to loose the chains of injustice
>   and untie the cords of the yoke,
> to set the oppressed free
>   and break every yolk?
> Is it not to share your food with the hungry
>   and to provide the poor wanderer with shelter—
> when you see the naked, to clothe him,
>   and not to turn away from your own flesh and blood?
> Then your light will break forth like the dawn,
>   and your healing will quickly appear;
> then your righteousness will go before you,
>   and the glory of the Lord will be your rear guard.
> Then you will call, and the Lord will answer;
>   you will cry for help, and he will say: Here I am.
> "If you do away with the yoke of oppression,
>   with the pointing finger and malicious talk, . . .

(And then come the verses that guided my father's life and ministry)

> *... and if you spend yourselves in behalf of the hungry*
> *and satisfy the needs of the oppressed,*
> *then your light will rise in the darkness,*
> *and your night will become like the noonday.*
> *"The Lord will guide you always;*
> *he will satisfy your needs in a sun-scorched land*
> *and will strengthen your frame.*
> *You will be like a well-watered garden,*
> *like a spring whose waters never fail."*

Isaiah concludes that those who take on the yoke of the needy

> *"... will rebuild the ancient ruins*
> *and will raise up the age-old foundations;*
> *you will be called Repairer of Broken Walls,*
> *Restorer of Streets with Dwellings" (Isa. 58:6–12).*

Every Christmas afternoon my dad did something that to me, as a boy consumed with my toys and newly accumulated bounty, seemed rather strange. It *was* strange then, but today it is one of my most treasured memories. A few blocks down the street lived an elderly widow who was often alone on Christmas Day. When my dad went to the closet to get his heavy winter coat and boots, I would ask where he was going. He replied that a lonely widow lived down the street, and he was going to wish her a merry Christmas and hoped to lift her spirits and pray with her.

This was the kind of thing my father did day after day as part of his ministry. A holiday should have exempted him from the responsibility of bearing other people's burdens. But for my dad, ministering to the needs of people was not a job—it was his way of living out Isaiah 58:10–11. I can't help but know that Christ felt loved as my dad shared space with the woman at Jesus' feet.

I am struck with Jesus' response when John the Baptist's disciples sent a group to check out His credentials. I would have expected Jesus to show a copy of his stellar accomplishments detailing His work as the creator of the universe or His position as the King of all Kings. But instead He responds,

> "Go back and report to John what you hear and see: The blind receive sight, the lame walk, those who have leprosy are cured, the deaf hear, the dead are raised, and the good news is preached to the poor. Blessed is the man who does not fall away on account of me" (Matt. 11:4–6).

When Jesus is asked to present His credentials, He says,

> *"The spirit of the Lord is on me,*
>   *because he has anointed me*
>   *to preach good news to the poor.*
> *He has sent me to proclaim freedom for the prisoners*
>   *and recovery of sight for the blind,*
> *to release the oppressed,*
>   *to proclaim the year of the Lord's favor" (Luke 4:18–19).*

Do you ever wonder what Christ would do if He reappeared in His post-resurrected form? I would hope that He might agree to speak at Moody's Founders Week. I would expect to hear that He was doing a preaching tour of America's great mega-churches. We might assume that stadiums would be jammed with tens of thousands to catch a glimpse of Him.

But I doubt that that is where He would spend most of His time. He would spend it walking the streets and alleys, looking for the poor, the disadvantaged, the hungry, the homeless, and those whom nobody else cares about.

If we are to love Christ, we have to learn to walk the streets with Him.

If we are to love Christ, we have to learn to walk
the streets with Him.

Eloise Peace and Jenny Matthews both work at Moody. Eloise cheers the employees from the grill in the lunchroom, and Jenny works in the mailroom. Eloise and Jenny spend their weekends in jail. But they are not serving time; they are serving Christ. Every weekend finds them leading Bible studies for the inmates. They open up the gyms of the jail for worship services with the inmates. Every Christmas they wrap hundreds of gifts to give to prisoners. Last Christmas Jenny and Eloise fed fourteen thousand prisoners with their bountiful home cooking. As phenomenal and self-sacrificing as all of this seems, it is really about two women touching Christ with their love.

One of my favorite experiences at Moody is to be on campus when the freshmen arrive. I particularly like to watch the mothers as they bring their precious cherubs to the big city of Chicago. Some of them appear to be frozen in fright and anxiety. I try to comfort them by saying, tongue in cheek, "Don't worry about your child—we only lost seven on the streets last year. And that was down from eighteen the year before!"

Yet an amazing thing happens over the four years these students are at Moody. Some of the students who come from rural areas end up loving the city—and not just its energy, recreation, and cultural events, but more importantly, its people.

A case in point is Glen Kehrein, who grew up in the backwoods of Wisconsin. At the end of his four years he moved to the despairing neighborhoods of the Austin communities on Chicago's West Side. He and his wife, Lonnie, took over a struggling, failing ministry and never left. Today Circle Urban Ministries shines as a lighthouse and a proof that some people can love Christ in very productive ways.

Two years ago I was with Glen at his ministry, and he took me to the new school CUM had just founded. Glen told me that if they have any hope of reaching their neighborhood, they have to reach these children at an early age. The parents can't afford to send them to the school, and most of them don't have fathers at home. These are the truly needy. I looked in their faces, heard them stand and recite Scripture, and thought how touched Christ must feel.

People like Glen and Eloise and Jenny are gifted, yet they pay a price for years of tough, unheralded labor. Not all of us are so called. But the tragedy of their ministries and so many others like them all over the world is that for the most part they do it alone. Chicago is surrounded with affluent suburbs where Christians spend their money, their evenings, and their weekends on themselves. Commuting Christians travel through some of the city's blighted neighborhoods in sleek, protective, fast-moving trains. Lost in the most recent headlines, we walk to our offices and back to our trains for another safe and shielded trip home. All the while we rarely notice the needs and rarely think about the faithful and few Glens who are showing their love to Christ on the very streets where His heart beats.

The greatest tragedy of all is that Glen cannot raise enough money to support the needs of the school and every year has to consider closing it. Just a small effort to love Christ in partnership with those who are doing street love would release amazing new potential in reaching both lives and neighborhoods for Christ. But it isn't happening.

I wonder how Christ feels about churches in the affluent suburbs that surround such desperate needs. We take great pride in sending expansive amounts of our money to meet needs in faraway lands and are, on occasion, even willing to send our sons and daughters. Yet the great opportunities to make a difference for Christ a few miles away go seemingly unnoticed and unappreciated.

This is why the thought of Christ examining our tax returns to see exactly what we have done to love the disadvantaged and the oppressed is such an unsettling thought.

One evening some friends took Martie and me to a restaurant noted for its big, thick, juicy steaks. As the waiter was describing the extensive selection of steaks, my eyes followed my stomach to the twenty-two-ounce offering. Since all the steaks cost the same, I knew it was my chance to prove my manly capacity. Not wanting to glance toward Martie lest she curb my savage instincts, I boldly ordered the "big one"! But I could only get about two-thirds of the way through it. I asked our server to wrap up the rest so I could take it home.

While the rest of the party went to the rest rooms, I waited outside. I noticed a homeless man approaching me with a copy of the *Streetwise* paper. The homeless in Chicago who are trying to rehabilitate themselves sell these small newspapers for a dollar. I didn't have a dollar. My smallest bill was a five-dollar bill, and as the man approached, I was determined not to part with that much money. I turned him down flat, and he kindly said, "God bless you, brother," and moved on.

At that moment I was convicted by the thought that I could indulge my appetite with a massive steak but couldn't muster the spiritual decency to meet this homeless man's needs. So I called him back and said that I wanted to give him my five-dollar bill in the name of Jesus who had given so much to save me.

The man didn't miss a beat. No sooner had he taken the bill than he said, "Do you need what's in the bag, too?"

That was the last straw. I informed him that I had plans for the leftovers. He thanked me and disappeared around the corner. My sense of conviction only grew worse. How could I have so much and be so begrudging to one who had so little? As Martie and our friends emerged from the restaurant, they watched me disappear around the corner, yelling, "Sir! Sir! Wait a minute! You can have the steak. Really! I want you to have it." They thought I had lost my mind until I shamefacedly explained.

I couldn't believe myself. I had just been working on this chapter, yet I was still out of touch with what it means to express love to Jesus.

If we say we love Christ, He will no doubt ask us when was the last time we fed the hungry, gave to the poor, clothed the naked, gave the thirsty something to drink, or visited those in prison. When we can answer that question with specific details about loving actions toward the disadvantaged, then we can believe we have touched Jesus with our love.

Unless, of course, we are more taken with own cash and comfort.

CHAPTER ELEVEN

BETRAYAL

Love at the Crossroads

She was an attractive young mother, probably thirty-something. After a meeting this past summer at a conference, she told me she had been a single parent for eleven years. She said that the hope of her heart had been that God would bring a man into her life who would restore the comfort of companionship and intimacy she longed for. Through the years she prayed that the Lord would bring her His man. She vowed not to step away from her commitment to Christ to make it happen. Her heart's desire was to love Christ more than the wrong man.

As she told me of her struggle, I could sense the tension rising in her heart. I have never known the loneliness and lack of companionship of being a single parent, but she was making it clear to me that raising a child alone is a tough and challenging experience.

She paused. Her head dropped as her feet nervously toed the ground. She confessed that recently her commitment to Christ had given in to her desire for a more comfortable way of life. Sadly she told me that for the last couple of years, men had come in and out of her life as though she were a revolving door. As tears rolled down her cheeks, she said, "Joe, I am so ashamed." When it came to a choice between Christ and comfort in her life, she ultimately opted for someone to make her comfortable.

Dan was an upwardly mobile corporate executive who worked for a national cable television company. He had oversight of all the regional outlets and was considered a "comer" in the industry. After church one Sunday, he approached me and said, "Pastor, I have to ask you a question because something is really troubling me. I've committed my life to serve Christ without reservation. But part of my work involves providing pornography through outlets from this cable company. I know that that part of my work is not honoring to Christ. What should I do?" To say that he should leave his job meant that he would place in jeopardy his affluence, the kind of upward mobility he desired, and not least of all, his family's means of livelihood. So we agreed to take the week to pray about it and to seek God's wisdom.

Francis Schaeffer observed, just before he died, that there were two dynamics that define and drive the modern American: affluence and personal peace. Or, to put it another way, cash and comfort.

Our desire to love Christ with the totality of our being is frequently on a collision course with the lure of cash and comfort.

We who are committed to becoming Christ-lovers will inevitably have to make a choice as to what will finally drive the agenda of our lives. Even well-intentioned followers find that our desire to love Him with the totality of our being is frequently on a collision course with the lure of cash and comfort.

You may be thinking, "What's the deal? Since when is there something wrong with cash and comfort?" True, cash and comfort are obviously among the best elixirs of life. But at some point we must decide whether or not they will be in charge of our lives. To place them in perspective, we must ask, "Is there anything more important than affluence and personal peace?" It is the old "compared with what?" question. Compared with poverty and pain, I am obsessed with cash and comfort. But compared with Christ? That is where we begin to feel the tension.

Life has a way of pushing us to the point of needing to decide whether the pursuit of earthly pleasure and treasure will be more important to us than a non-negotiated love for Christ. The decision is not without consequence. When we are forced to make a choice, we discover that a choice for anything instead of Christ inevitably leads us to betray Him.

Christ taught us that we can love only one master. We will either love Christ or love the secondary stuff this world has to offer. The choice is clear and decisive. There is no middle ground. And in case you are thinking that loving Christ consigns us to a life of abject poverty and suffering, we must remember that God takes pleasure in blessing His own. In fact, He consistently proves that He is a generous God. Everything He gives us is a gift of grace. Loving Him simply means that He is first among everything else, and that if we have to make a choice, we will always choose Him.

CASH OR CHRIST

The tendency to let cash and comfort eclipse our love for Christ is not always as blatant as the pressures of living without love or giving up a promising career. Usually the choices are far more subtle. We may be tempted toward the small, seemingly inconsequential decision to tell a "white" lie to keep some uncomfortable consequences at bay, or make a slight compromise in the marketplace to give our financial bottom line a slight advantage. After all, don't we all need to have a little space to maneuver life to work toward our best interests? Well, maybe. But if the maneuvering means cheating on Christ, the edges soon erode. What begins as a small flirtation, a lingering thought, the luxury of a slip here and there kicks open the door to betrayals on increasingly larger scales. Judas, who holds the all-time record for betrayal, didn't wake up one morning and say, "I think that I'll trade Christ in for thirty pieces of silver!"

Compromising Christ for either cash or comfort puts us in bad company. It may make us uncomfortable to think that we have something in common with Judas, but this is one time when a little discomfort might work to our advantage. Judas is obviously not our favorite guy. He's the worst scoundrel of Scripture, the one who treacherously turned Jesus over to men who couldn't wait to crucify Him. The very name repulses us—have you ever heard parents choosing a name for their baby say, "We like the name Judas . . . or Judas Anne . . . it has a cute ring to it!" We distance ourselves from Judas as though we could never do what he did. But if we think we could never share space with Judas, we should think again.

John 13 paints the backdrop to Judas's betrayal and helps us understand how someone so intimately connected to Christ and seemingly a committed lover of Christ could so calculatedly and coldly betray Him. The chapter takes us to the Upper Room where Christ is gathered with His disciples as His three-year ministry with them nears an end.

Jesus, longing to eat the Passover with them, had sent John and Peter to find a room where they could celebrate the feast. Having found the place, they lead Jesus and the disciples through the crowded city streets that are buzzing with the usual excitement of the Passover festivities. As the crowd presses forward to get a glimpse of Jesus, the small entourage disappears through a doorway. As the door shuts behind them, the street noise dissipates into the sound of the shuffling of sandals up the worn stone stairs. Their entrance into the room marks the beginning of one of Jesus' most intimate exchanges with His disciples. The disciples must be sensing again, as they no doubt often have, the unusual privilege of having been chosen to be so closely connected with the One who has attracted so much attention and has captured the heart of the masses.

We all know about the Upper Room. This Last Supper has marked our own memories with thoughts of footwashing, communion, and Jesus' preparing the disciples for life without Him through the teachings we know as the "Upper Room discourse." We who gather at the Lord's Table to celebrate communion often find our minds reflecting back as though we were there at the table with Him when He broke the bread and passed the wine. What often escapes our notice, however, is the fact that Judas was there as well, having already initiated his plan to betray Jesus later that night.

But John had not forgotten about Judas. When John described the occasion of the Last Supper, he clearly had Judas on his mind. And wouldn't you? Imagine the shock to an unsuspecting group of disciples that one who had been so loved and blessed of Christ could turn his heart so quickly, so brutally, so shamefully against Jesus. Betrayal would be the last thing they would suspect.

Leonardo da Vinci's masterpiece *The Last Supper,* which depicts a long table with all the disciples sitting on one side, is obviously a concession to the artist's need to paint all their faces. That is not the way they were. At a dinner like this, the tables would have been set in a "U" shape, two tables at the sides and one at the end. Five disciples would be placed down one side and five on the other. That left the center table for Jesus, with a disciple on each side of Him. To the right of Jesus was John, the beloved disciple who is leaning back on the bosom of Christ. But it is interesting that most scholars believe Judas was the one positioned to the left of Christ—and the left side of the host was the place of highest honor. As the disciples are gathered at this intimate meal, away from the crowds, Jesus is making a point as He intentionally invites Judas to occupy the place of honor.

John opens his story of the events of the evening with this striking statement:

> It was just before the Passover Feast. Jesus knew that the time had come for him to leave this world and go to the Father. Having loved his own who were in the world, he now showed them the full extent of his love (John 13:1).

I love this about Jesus. John says that as He prepares to move into the most agonizing season of His time on this earth—we could hardly blame Him if He were self-focused and wanting the comfort, support, and even pity of His closest friends—He never stopped loving His own.

John interrupts the flow of that wonderful thought of Christ's enduring love by telling us, "The evening meal was being served, and the devil had already prompted Judas Iscariot, son of Simon, to betray

Jesus" (v. 2). John is clearly impressed that the most unusual thing that happened, the thing he can never forget, is Judas's turning against Jesus.

Perhaps John is struck with the fact that Judas is probably the last one he would have suspected as a betrayer. Luke's gospel relates that, as was often the case when they met together, the disciples got into a discussion of who was going to be the greatest among them when Christ established the kingdom. Judas's name would be on the table in a discussion like that because he was the treasurer. As such, he was obviously trusted by Christ and the others. Moreover, on this night Judas was seated in the place of honor. Even doubting Thomas would not have doubted Judas's credentials.

As the disciples banter about who are going to be the big shots in the kingdom, Jesus, in a beautiful picture of His enduring love, gets up from the table, takes off His robes, and places a towel around His waist—a sign that He was going to wash their feet. This is what the house servant would have done. Imagine: God takes the form of a servant and washes all of their feet as if to say, "The kingdom is not about who's the big shot. The kingdom is about which one of us will be willing to humble himself and serve." Judas was among those whose feet were washed by Jesus.

The foot–washing over, John relates,

> After he had said this, Jesus was troubled in spirit and testified, "I tell you the truth, one of you is going to betray me." His disciples stared at one another, at a loss to know which of them he meant (John 13:21–22).

What a riveting moment this is! The disciples are frozen in shock and disbelief. Staring at each other, they look for body language to reveal the identity of the culprit. Did Thomas's eyes twitch when Jesus said that? Did anyone blush or squirm uncomfortably?

There are no clues, so Peter whispers to John to ask Jesus who it is. Leaning back, John asks the Lord, "Who is it?" Jesus answers, "It is the one to whom I will give this piece of bread when I have dipped it in the dish" (v. 26). At this point Jesus tears off a piece of bread and dips it into a special mixture of raisins, dates, and sour wine, a sauce reserved for special feasts such as this. In that Jewish culture, to receive a morsel dipped in this sauce from the host was to be highly honored. So Jesus has not only seated Judas in the place of honor but also now affirms His love for the one who has plotted to betray Him.

We would think that Judas's heart would wilt under the pressure of Jesus' undeserving love for him. But that is not the case. Sometimes our hearts are determined to betray Christ regardless. A heart that is impervious to the abounding love of Christ is a cold heart indeed.

John continues,

> Then, dipping the piece of bread, he gave it to Judas Iscariot, son of Simon. As soon as Judas took the bread, Satan entered into him.
> "What you are about to do, do quickly," Jesus told him, but no one at the meal understood why Jesus said this to him. Since Judas had charge of the money, some thought Jesus was telling him to buy what was needed for the Feast, or to give something to the poor. As soon as Judas had taken the bread, he went out. And it was night (John 13:26–30).

The apostle John is infatuated with metaphors of light and dark. His writings are full of these images. For John, light always represents Jesus, the Light of the World. The kingdom of Satan is always described in terms of darkness or night. I believe John makes it a point to say that it was night as an image of Judas's entrance into the dark kingdom of the adversary.

This is an incredulous development in the story of these followers of Christ. One wonders how a disciple who has walked with God for three years, has seen the miracles, and is the object of His intimate affection, grace, and love could do such a thing. How could one who so personally feels God's touch, has listened to the depths of Jesus' wisdom, has witnessed the compassion on even the worst of sinners—how could he betray Jesus and hand Him over to the authorities, knowing that they would seek to have Him crucified? Do you consider this strange? I do. What would ever drive Judas to do this?

Before we try to answer that question, let us consider what it takes to make life choices that betray Christ's love for us. Judas reflects at least three dynamics of a betrayer's heart.

BETRAYAL IS ALWAYS AN INSIDE-OUT MATTER

The shocking thing is that, as we have seen, Judas was the last person you would have expected to betray Jesus. He was the treasurer, entrusted with all the funds of the kingdom. The rest of the disciples, having watched him closely for three years, had great respect for him. When Jesus handed him the morsel and Judas left, none of them said, "That figures! We knew Judas would ultimately do something like this. It was just a matter of time." The disciples were clueless.

When it comes to betrayal, our external façade is irrelevant, regardless of position, honor, gifts, or capabilities. It doesn't matter whether people look up to you and applaud your achievements. Betraying Christ is always about what's going on in the unseen world of our hearts. Whether we betray Him in small or big ways, whether we have a high profile or are relatively unnoticed, it's always the same. It never becomes obvious until we have first compromised our hearts.

I recently shared the platform at a Bible Conference in Hong Kong with one of Great Britain's most brilliant and gifted expositors. He had emerged as the leader of the new generation of evangelicals in the United Kingdom. Martie and I feasted on his marvelous teaching from the book of Ruth. The brief times of fellowship that we had together were a treasure. His books have helped and supported my own teaching ministry.

You can imagine my disbelief a few months later when I learned that my partner in ministry in Hong Kong had left his wife, his family, and his church. He had left them to be with the young man he traveled with. Just after hearing the sad news, I opened the *London Times* to see a large picture of him and a headline story of his departure from his home and ministry. He had not only betrayed his wife and those who trusted and followed his ministry, but now he had publicly defamed Christ and the cause that he had served so effectively.

None of us is exempt from cultivating a heart condition on the inside that will inevitably show up on the outside in tragic ways. Some of us have already betrayed Christ in our hearts. The outward expression of that betrayal is not the first and foremost act. Betrayal is an attitude formed and framed on the inside. Judas had decided to betray Jesus long before he acted on the attitude of his heart.

BETRAYAL COMES IN THE FACE OF HIS LOVE

Not only is betrayal an inside-out matter, but it is always done *in the face of Christ's love.* Consider that Jesus has loved Judas for three years, and now, in their last evening together, Jesus has intentionally given him a seat of honor, has washed his feet, and has intentionally and lovingly shared with him the morsel of bread as if to say, "I know that you are going to betray me, but even that can't erase my love for you." I find myself asking Judas, why? If Jesus had treated you badly, maybe you would want to turn on Him. But how can you betray in the face of such phenomenal love?

> *When we betray Christ, we have to do it in the face of His amazing love for us. That's what makes it so wrong, so brazen, so arrogant.*

We need to think about that as well. Are we ever tempted to betray Christ for personal pleasure or gain? Look into His face. He has loved you the way no one has ever loved you. Look at the nail scars in His hands—they are there for your sake. Think of His grace. Look at His daily provision. And what of the mercy He extends to you every day. When we betray Christ, we have to do it in the face of His amazing love for us. That's what makes it so wrong, so brazen, so arrogant.

One weekend Martie was at our daughter's home caring for a newborn grandchild and I wasn't scheduled to preach, so I decided to worship at Fellowship Baptist Church. This church, or "The Ship" as it is affectionately called, is one of the leading African-American churches in Chicago. Its pastor, Dr. Clay Evans, who founded the church fifty years ago, is a nationally recognized preacher.

The best part of the service was Dr. Evans's message, based on the passage in John 18 where Pilate, after interrogating Jesus, comes back out to the crowd and says, "I find no fault in Him." As only a black preacher can do, he began to wax eloquent with the phrase. He noted that we live in a world with no-fault divorce and no-fault insurance, yet most of us find fault with just about everything else. He reminded us, through a chorus of "all right," "don't stop now," and "well, preacher" responses from the congregation, that there are people who come to church looking to find fault with this, that, or the other thing. We can always find fault with our boss, our parents, and our government. But, Dr. Evans concluded, "When I see Jesus, I find no fault in Him." Evans went on to extrapolate in golden tones that he found no fault in His love, in His mercy, in His grace, in His Word, or in His Spirit.

It was a marvelous sermon. As Dr. Evans finished, he reminded the much-involved congregation that if they would take a close look at Christ, they would find no fault in Him as well. It is a wonderful thought. We have and are loved by a no-fault Jesus. If you and I choose to betray Him, we will have to betray Him in the face of His faultless love for us. He has never given us a reason to betray Him. That is something we have to think about.

BETRAYAL IS STUBBORN

When we compare the accounts of the Judas story in the various Gospels, it becomes clear that by the time the disciples get to the Upper Room, Judas has already cut the deal and made up his mind. He has been to the authorities and has negotiated a price. Then, at the Last Supper, Jesus honors him with a distinguished seat, washes his feet, and shares a morsel of bread. We can imagine that Judas's resolve was being challenged, not by condemnation or a public harangue, but by the strong love of Christ. Even when Jesus predicts—and in essence tells Judas that He knows—what he is going to do, Judas gets up and goes out to do the deed anyway. I couldn't believe how stubborn Judas was until I read my own heart.

When we have decided that we want to sin, that the wrong in our lives serves some purpose that is more important than anything else, we have the capacity to dig in and insulate our choice from any outside influence that would cause us to change. We go to church and essentially say to God, "I don't care what You or anyone else says today. I don't plan on changing the wrong things in my life. I don't care what my spouse says, what my friends say. I don't care what it means to my job, to my family, or even to the reputation of Christ." The resolve to sin and to continue in its ways is an engine that is powerful enough to drive us past even the deepest love of Christ all the way to betrayal if we want it to. Betraying Christ in our lives will always be an inside-out, in-His-face, stubborn enterprise.

But what could be the reason that Judas takes this tragic step? Where did it all start?

The answer is simple. The answer lies in the choices that Judas made. I have said it before, but I can't escape the profound nature of the insight that a friend shared with me many years ago. As we sat on the sprawling porch of a lodge in the mountains of upstate New York, he said, "Joe, I'm convinced that our lives are made not of the dreams we dream, but of the choices we make." It was Judas's choices that made his life—choices that ultimately turned what he thought were best for him—into sorrow and despair.

It was Judas's choices that made his life—choices
that ultimately turned what he thought were best
for him—into sorrow and despair.

Now, we might conclude that Judas is actually a victim of Satan's design on his life. John does say that the devil had already put this in Judas's heart (John 13:2) and that after Judas received the morsel, Satan entered into him (v. 27). That might make us think that Judas is little more than a pawn in a cosmic struggle between God and Satan.

In case we are tempted to think Satan can overcome us against our will, we need to be reminded of what God's Word says about our choices to sin. James tells us that we sin when we are led by our own fallen desires; then when we are led astray by misguided desire, that desire produces sin; finally, when sin is triggered, it brings forth death (James 1:14–15).

The comedian Flip Wilson used to do a sketch in which his colorful character Geraldine comes home with an expensive new dress. She tries it on for her husband, who immediately asks why she bought it, since they don't have the money to pay for it. Geraldine responds, "The devil made me do it." To which her husband replies, "Why didn't you tell Satan to get behind you?" "I did," Geraldine responds, "and he said it looks good from back here, too."

The excuse may have worked for Geraldine's husband, but it won't work with God. We are accountable for all our sin. Our choices cultivate the soil of our hearts to be receptive to the toxic weeds that Satan sows in our lives.

What were the choices that led Judas to betray Jesus? John's gospel gives us clues in chapter twelve. The scene is set in the home of Lazarus just after Jesus' miracle of raising Lazarus from the dead. Needless to say, these are happy days in the town of Bethany. The resurrection was a truly amazing miracle. Now, because of the loving power of Christ, Mary and Martha have their brother back. Jesus is there along with all the disciples. At this high point in Jesus' ministry, the family of Lazarus is ecstatic and the air resonates with celebration and joy.

Lost in love and gratitude, Mary, the sister of Lazarus, brings to the feet of Jesus what would have been her most prized possession. Her gift to Jesus is a pound of spikenard, a perfume of the most expensive kind. This treasure was worth a year's wages. For Mary there are not enough words to say thank you for what Jesus has done. So, like the woman of Luke 7, she expresses her thanks in the nonverbal language of taking her best and bringing it to Jesus' feet as an act of worship and love. Because she is surrounded by many others who love Christ, we can be sure that everyone else in the room is "amen-ing" the profound meaning of the moment. Everyone, that is, except Judas. Judas, sounding pious and compassionate, asks, "Why wasn't this perfume sold and the money given to the poor?"

Beware when people sound too spiritual.

John reveals that Judas's real motive in complaining about a missed opportunity to be generous lies in the fact that he is a thief and has often stolen from the till. If the spikenard had been taken and sold and not "wasted," Judas, the trusted treasurer, would have a windfall to manage for his own gain. It now becomes clear that Judas made a choice early on that he would not be in this disciple thing for Christ and Christ alone, but that he would be in it for the cash. Jesus and this kingdom trip He was on would be for the personal benefit of Judas. "A little more cash" was the motive behind Judas's choices. Just think: If Jesus established His kingdom on the earth and overthrew the Roman government, guess who would be head of the Department of the Treasury? Judas! Guess who's going to get to embezzle tons of money? Judas!

At some point in time, Judas made a choice that his life would revolve around money. Cash would rule his life. He would evaluate everything through dollar signs. His ethics would be dictated by personal gain.

But the deeper question is, why betray Jesus? In the last few weeks before His death, Jesus began preparing the disciples for the fact that He was going to die. He was informing them that the social and political revolution they had all anticipated was not coming to pass—at least not yet. The news that he would not be the treasurer in the new Israeli government would have shattered Judas's dreams of wealth and gain. If Jesus is headed for the cross, Judas's stealth enterprise has no future. There is no doubt that at this point he cuts a deal with the leaders who sought Jesus' head. At least Judas can get another thirty pieces of silver before his dreams evaporate. And that is why he betrays Jesus. When the choice is between cash or Christ, Judas chooses the cash.

This leads us to the second reason that Judas betrays Jesus. After Jesus announces to the disciples that He is going to the cross, He warns them that they, too, are going to suffer for His name. Jesus tells them that they are going to be kicked out of the synagogue. Their families are going to disown them. And some of them will die for His sake. Immediately after Jesus makes this announcement, Judas goes to the authorities and plots with them behind closed doors (Mark 13:9–13). It seems apparent that Judas is not only in this thing for cash, but he's in it for comfort as well. If it's going to mean suffering and sacrifice, then he's out of there.

So Judas gets the thirty pieces of silver and stays in control of the comfort factor in his life. These were the choices that drove Judas's betrayal.

A HOLE BURNED IN JUDAS'S HEART

If you were to look at Judas at this stage of his life, he would look like a smashing success. You can almost see him sitting at Bennie's Bistro in some posh neighborhood of Jerusalem, sipping a latte at the sidewalk café. Maybe he's thinking about this weekend, when he will be able to go to his penthouse condo overlooking the beaches in Tel Aviv. All the while he's feeling sorry for those other eleven guys who are groveling for their last meal and being kicked out of synagogues. If all we had were this part of the saga, we might think that betrayal pays. But we need to look at the rest of the story.

I am reminded of the words of Peter Berger in his book *A Rumor of Angels*.

> He who sups with the devil had better have a long spoon, because he who sups with the devil will find that his spoon gets shorter and shorter until that last supper in which he is left alone at the table with no spoon at all and an empty

plate. But the devil, one may guess, will have by then gone
on to more interesting company.[1]

Matthew 27 gives us a gripping look at the last chapter of Judas's
life. Judas, standing afar off, sees Jesus, hands bound, surrounded by
Roman guards, being led to the trial. Judas had seen those hands before.
He had seen them still the sea and touch the blind and lame. How often
those hands had touched Judas with His love! An arm around his shoul-
der. A pat on the back. A wave. A handshake. A passing of the sop dipped
in the rich Passover sauce. But now he sees Jesus' hands bound and his
loving leader condemned to die.

Judas's heart is struck with deep, penetrating sorrow. The sorrow
is so heavy that the thirty pieces of silver no longer seem a reward but
the symbol of his misery. With every step, their clanging becomes a
dirge of condemnation. When he sees what he has done, Judas hates
the cash he has craved so much and takes the money back to the authorities. They tell him in no uncertain terms that they do not want the
money back, and in an act of desperation Judas flings the money into
the sanctuary and runs.

When I was a boy, my dad, observing my spendthrift ways, often
said that money burned a hole in my pocket. These thirty pieces of silver burned a hole in Judas's heart. When you and I make choices to
betray Christ, sooner or later the outcome of that betrayal will fill our
lives with sorrow. The things we have gained at Christ's expense and the
comforts we have enjoyed by resisting sacrifice and suffering for Him
will all turn to symbols of our sorrow.

*"There is a way that seems right to a man, but in
the end it leads to death."*

Where can Judas turn now? What is he to do? I am reminded of
the Old Testament saying, "There is a way that seems right to a man,
but in the end it leads to death" (Prov. 14:12; 16:25).

Judas's sorrow is so overwhelming, the predicament he has created so dreadfully impossible to unravel, that he goes out and takes his own life. That, too, was a choice—he didn't have to do that. At the moment when he locks eyes with Jesus, he could have said, "Lord, I've failed You so deeply. I'm such a sinner. Could You find the mercy in Your heart to forgive me?" He could have done that, and Jesus' answer would have been, "Yes!" Jesus consistently proves to us that He is indeed a friend of sinners, even sinners who have offended Him most deeply.

But Judas, so locked in his own system, so overcome by his own failure, feels he has only one option, and that is to end it all.

For us, betraying Christ in lesser ways may not lead to suicide, but there will be consequences. Francis Schaeffer puts it well in writing about 1 Corinthians 3. In that chapter we read that at the end of our lives, we will be led before Christ. In a very powerful metaphor, the text says that what we have built in our lives—wood, hay, stubble, gold, silver, precious stones—will be tried by fire. The wood, hay, and stubble are not necessarily evil deeds, just worthless things that don't count for eternity.

When we come before Christ, the blazing fire of His glory will burn away all the wood, hay, and stubble. Only those things done for Christ and for eternity will remain. They will be the gold, silver, and precious stones the text speaks of, and we will be able to present these remaining works to Christ in worship and service at His feet. Schaeffer says that on that day there will be many "ash heap Christians." They will stand before the Lord, having all the stuff that didn't count for eternity burned away. In the end they will be knee-deep in the ashes with nothing to present to Him.

We who share space with Judas, who betray Christ for lesser things, will sadly identify with the closing scene of the movie *Schindler's List*. In the powerful climax to the story, Schindler, who had once been a wealthy businessman, says farewell to a group of Jews he has delivered from the Holocaust at great personal sacrifice. Suddenly he is gripped with the fact that he's standing by his big, beautiful car. He looks at the car and says, "I could have done more. I should have sold this car. It would have been ten more if I sold this car. This pen—it would have been five more. I could have gotten five more for this pen. This ring—the gold in this ring. I could have gotten two, no maybe one for this ring." The scene closes with him weeping because he could have done more.

I think that when the very best of us stand before Christ, we will say that we could have done more. Knowing this in advance, we should resolve that if Christ pushes against our cash and our comfort, we will choose Christ every time.

With tears running down her cheeks, that single parent of the two-year-old girl told me that she was so ashamed. She said she had decided to reclaim the ground in her life and never betray Christ again for personal comfort. If she had to choose between the wrong man in her life and Christ, it would be Christ. If necessary, she would make the sacrifice. She would love Him more than her own desires.

Dan came to me the next Sunday and said that he had resigned from his job with the cable company. It immediately crossed my mind that God had probably miraculously answered our prayer by providing another job for Dan. I asked him to tell me about his new job, but he replied that he didn't have one. He had no idea what he was going to do, but he knew that he could not deny Christ in his life. His immediate plans were to move in with his in-laws until he could figure out what to do.

Dan had to make a choice—and he chose Christ. I saw Dan about eight years later, and he told me that if he had to do it over again he would still make the same choice. I wondered where he might be today if he had made the choice to stay and reap the rewards of a skyrocketing career. If I understand the principle of betrayal, he would not be better off. Not really.

So if you have to make a choice between loving cash and comfort and loving Christ, ask the single parent which to choose. Ask Dan. More importantly, ask Judas. They will tell you to love Christ every time.

It will be worth it all when we see Jesus.
Life's trials will seem small when we see Him.
One glimpse of His dear face all sorrows will erase.
So bravely run the race 'til we see Christ.

Several months ago on a flight to the West Coast, a young man named Keith approached me and introduced himself. In the course of our conversation, I asked him what he did for a living. Keith said he was a consultant with a firm that serves the major Fortune 500 companies in the area of strategic planning and corporate training. I told him that we were looking for a corporate trainer at Moody and asked him for his card. I had my doubts that he would want to leave his Fortune 500 connections for Moody, since there would be no way that we could compete with the salary he was currently earning.

I gave his card to the head of our human resources department. It was, I said, at least worth a call. Keith now heads up our corporate training department. I saw him a few weeks ago and reminded him of our conversation on the plane. I told him I was so thankful that he had come to serve Christ at Moody and knew that this was a huge sacrifice, given the salary he had been making. I will never forget what Keith said to me. "It really was not a sacrifice at all. I have always told Christ that He would be first in my life, and now I finally got the opportunity to prove it."

I call that loving Christ in a powerful and profound way.

At the crossroads, when it is clear that loving Christ means giving up the allure of affluence and personal peace, choose Christ. It's a choice you will never regret.

CHAPTER TWELVE

AFTER THE PARTY

Loving Christ When Life Goes Back to Normal

It would be wonderful to envision living the rest of our lives next to the woman at Jesus' feet. But life rarely permits extended seasons of such moving experiences. Good times don't last forever. Life has a way of getting in the face of our well-meaning intentions. Early morning moments with Christ soon give way to the reality of the office with all of its stress and problems. Days are full of the reality of people who make demands on us, disappoint us, manipulate and abuse us, distract and disappoint us. There are spouses who don't share our commitment to a life directed and motivated by love for Christ. There are parents who face the task of refereeing preschoolers and running nose patrol. Not only do difficulties and discouragement challenge our love for Him, but a myriad of seductions from this world threaten to come between us and an ongoing love-filled life with Christ.

The challenge was no different for our heroine.

At some point she, too, had to rise to her feet and make her way through the stunned crowd that no doubt parted in awe after her gutsy performance. But once outside Simon's house, it was back to the streets, where she would face the realities of her new life in radical transition.

For her it could never again be life as it had been. Her encounter with Jesus was far too profound. Some experiences are so significant that we never recover from them. For her, this was such an encounter. Now that Jesus had forgiven her, the streets where she once marketed her trade would now be the neighborhood where she would live out her love for Christ. Her life would never be the same again.

But that transformation held awkward and uncomfortable realities for her. Could she ever live down her reputation in the face of a cynical and disbelieving public? What of her former customers? What would she do now to reinvent her life in the context of loving the One who had so spectacularly delivered her? And what of life two, three, five years later when she would grow accustomed to the grace that had so powerfully released her? We never hear of this woman again in Scripture, but it seems safe to assume that the love for Christ she demonstrated in Simon's house continued to guide and define her for the rest of her life.

After all we have considered in this book, only one question remains: Does a grateful love guide and define your life? Or to put it another way, if you were charged for the crime of loving Christ, would there be enough evidence to convict you?

If we have been forgiven much, then we, like the woman, must permit our love for Christ to reinvent our lives. True lovers of Christ never succumb to the tendency to segment life into compartments of disconnected experiences. My job over there . . . a little money in this corner . . . secret failures and sins enjoyed behind this door . . . jaunts into leisure land down this hall . . . and on occasion a loving reflection on Christ. After which it is back to life as usual.

THE LOOK OF LOVE

If we are not careful, our love for Christ can become merely another slice of life instead of an all-consuming reality that controls all of life. And that is the very challenge we face day by day. A genuine love for Christ should provide the power to transform our response to everything and everybody in our world, regardless of how hostile or difficult. It is a power that can chase away the seductive lure of lusts, a power able to revolutionize the private world of our thoughts, fantasies, and dreams. Our love for Christ dictates the grid through which we decide how we use our time, money, and other precious resources. Nothing intimidates a true love for Christ—unless we let our love for lesser things shove aside our love for Him.

A genuine love for Christ should provide the power to transform our response to everything and everybody in our world, regardless of how hostile or difficult.

Those who have been forgiven much love Christ with an all-consuming all-transforming energy. Christ-lovers never give in to the notion that Sunday doesn't affect Monday. A true love for Christ transforms Monday, the workplace, our homes, our relationships, our addictions, our portfolios, and our good times as well as bad.

The ultimate question is, Do you want this kind of life? Let's face it, it's not really much of a question. If we are among the forgiven, we instinctively desire to live to love Him. To say that this kind of life is not for us is to admit a gross lack of understanding of and appreciation for what He has done for us.

So, for all of us who say Yes, the first issue is not, How do I let Christ know how much I love Him in every segment of my life? As important as that is, the first step toward a life transformed by love is learning to stay in love with Him.

My early skirmishes with romantic intrigues began when I decided that girls were more attractive to me than the elementary school pledge I had made with friends never to like or, more importantly, kiss any girl. Something remarkable happened in junior high. Girls changed . . . or was it I? Early experiences found my heart attracted to a particular girl this week and another the next. I would hear that Alice "liked" me, which would immediately catch my interest. By the time I sent the message back through a network of my friends and hers that I liked her as well, she was usually on to someone else. So I would send word down the line that I liked Barbara, and after a couple of days the word returned that she was interested. But by then, Kathy had stolen my heart.

This kind of random, fickle love can characterize our love for Christ. We love Him when we need Him or when we receive abounding gifts of grace. Yet in the normal pace of everyday existence it is more often our wealth and dreams and plans and earthly relationships that tug at our hearts.

Later in my life I fell in love with Martie. This was serious business now. I began to think that I could—should—marry her. It was time to grow up and learn not only what real love was all about but to learn how to cultivate that love and stay in love . . . for the rest of my life.

STAYING IN LOVE

In His most graphic instructions about the essence of a thriving relationship with Him, Christ commands us to "remain in my love" (John 15:9). He pictures us as branches intimately connected to Him, the vine. This connectedness is the key to our usefulness and fruitfulness as well as our ultimate source of satisfaction. As branches remain in the vine, remaining in His love is exactly what Christ-lovers set their hearts to do.

Abiding, as the King James Version puts it, is about *staying* in love with Christ. It is not temporary, transient, periodic, or dictated by external circumstances or influences. It is important to see this as a choice. For us, falling in love and staying in love is often determined by our emotions, experiences, and fulfilled or unfulfilled expectations. C. S. Lewis notes that it would be impossible to live in the fever of first-found love, in that state of "being in love," when he writes,

> Being in love is a good thing, but it is not the best thing. It is a noble feeling, but still a feeling. . . . Who could bear to

live in this excitement for even five years? But of course, ceasing to "be in love" need not mean ceasing to love. Love in a second sense, love as distinct from being in love, is not merely a feeling. It is a deep unity, maintained by the will and deliberately strengthened by habit; reinforced by the grace which both partners ask and receive from God. They can have this love for each other even at those moments when they do not like each other; as you love yourself even when you do not like yourself. They can retain this love even when each would easily, if they allowed themselves, "be in love" with someone else. "Being in love" first moved you to promise fidelity; this quieter love enables you to keep the promise.[1]

It is this kind of steady committed love that Christ is calling us to. It is a love that is characterized in John 15 by intentionality, reciprocity, and boundaries.

Being *intentional* about loving Christ is not a one-time decision. It is a decision we make many times a day. We make this decision while driving in traffic, in what we choose to think or not to think, in what we do with our money, our relationships, our time, and our energy. Every life choice is about staying in love with Christ.

Abiding in his love is also *reciprocal*. Vines and branches reciprocate in the relationship. The vine is the source of strength, supply, nourishment, and support. The branch bears fruit for the benefit and the glory of the vine. And the branch finds joy and satisfaction in fulfilling its purpose.

Christ teaches us that fruit is the sign that genuine abiding has taken place. When we stay in love with Christ in every choice, action, and attitude, we will be fruitful for Him and a blessing to others. For instance, choosing to love Christ by loving those who offend us triggers the fruit of forgiveness. That in turn glorifies His character and blesses those who receive our gift of forgiveness.

When we stay in love with Christ in every choice,
action, and attitude, we will be fruitful for Him
and a blessing to others.

But lest we be tempted to congratulate ourselves, it must be underscored that we do not forgive on our own. We do it for Christ because we love Him more than we hate our enemies. It is what He asks us to do, and He gives us the opportunity to make a statement to Him. Nor can we forgive without having been forgiven by Him first or without having the grace to obey that only He as the vine supplies. He supplies the direction; we obey. He is glorified and others are blessed. But it takes love to make it all happen—His love for us and our love for Him.

Even the ability to respond to His love must be seen as a gift of His grace. Scripture makes it clear that all we do comes by His gracious enablement. The apostle Paul, who of all people was eminently successful in responding to Christ's love in his life, admitted that everything he did came solely by God's grace: "By the grace of God I am what I am, and his grace to me was not without effect. No, I worked harder than all of them—yet not I, but the grace of God that was with me" (1 Cor. 15:10).

We must rely on God's grace in order to lovingly respond to Jesus. If we could manufacture the capacity to do anything apart from Him, pride would consume our spirit. It is like expressing our love to someone very special with an expensive, well-thought-out gift. After it is given, we feel a need to be recognized for what we have done. It's the old "Who loves ya, baby" need to be praised for the love we have shown. What was intended to be an expression of love ends up being about us. Again.

The reason that it is so hard to get this reciprocal love up and running in our hearts may very well be that we are trying to respond to Christ in our own strength. A living love for Him is a gift of His grace, and it is not a gift with which He is stingy or selective. He desires our love and freely enables us to engage it in our hearts. One of my favorite hymns has the line, "O for grace to trust Him more." If I had written the hymn, I would have wanted to sing, "O for grace to love Him more." A top priority in our daily prayer must be the heartfelt plea that God will grant us grace to love Him more.

Grace also provides the motivation to love. My constant awareness that I have been forgiven much is a credit to His grace. If it weren't for grace, forgiveness would not be in God's vocabulary. It is the appreciation of His saving grace that gets me up off my knees to search for ways to love Him more. And it is His Word and will that define what this love will look like in everyday life.

LIVING LOVINGLY

What would life look like if we were to take up permanent residence in the center of His love?

Our lives would never again be ordinary or predictable. Love has a way of making ordinary people do unordinary things. Christ-lovers do many things the world would consider unusual. We give our money away. We forgive deep and cruel injustices. We see people as more important than material possessions or personal dreams and desires. We ignore barriers of race, class, and culture to embrace the worth of others who are not like us. We accept and serve other followers of Christ regardless of what they are like or how they treat us. We refuse promotions and job transfers because they conflict with our capacity to serve Him and all that He has put in our charge. We love our spouses with sensitivity and sacrifice because that is how Christ loves us. We are willing to give up comfort and security to go to the remote and difficult places on the globe. And while we can't leap tall buildings with a single bound, we do supernaturally endure suffering and persecution all the way to the arena filled with lions or to the fiery stake.

Love has a way of making ordinary people do unordinary things. Christ-lovers do many things the world would consider unusual.

I am aware that for many of us to think of suffering as an act of love or to ponder the pain of persecution for Jesus is a huge disconnect. Yet we must remember that while we are reading these words in the comfort of our well-ordered world, brothers and sisters in many places are right now making these kinds of tough love choices. In China, Cuba, Iran, and the Sudan the ongoing persecution of Christians is well documented. In the southern half of Sudan Christians are being systematically executed daily—some crucified, others loaded into trucks to be dumped in the desert without provisions, to starve death. Their children are routinely rounded up and taken to major cities of the north to be sold as slaves. Before they are sold, they must convert to Islam.

Just two weeks ago a friend of mine who works in Islamic fields told of a friend of his who was in Khartoum, the capital city of Sudan. His friend watched as a group of several hundred of these children were gathered into the city square. The mullah came out of the mosque and commanded that all the children bow down and pray after him a prayer of conversion to Islam. All the children bowed except one. He was about nine years old, and when asked why he didn't bow down, he simply said he couldn't because he was a child of Jesus Christ. The angry mullah told him to fall down or he would be shot. The child refused, and the mullah ordered the guards to open fire.

As the boy fell to the ground, about forty other children stood to their feet in an expression of their allegiance to Christ. The mullah ordered four of them shot as well. As they fell to the ground, none of the others moved. The mullah was by now so distraught that he yelled, "You are not worthy to be slaves," and ordered the children who were still standing to be hauled away to prison.

Any love choice that I make for Christ pales in insignificance alongside the courageous love expressed by these young soldiers of the cross. It is hard to complain or wince at what He might demand in the light of such moving testimony to the worthiness of loving Christ regardless. I am reminded of the verse in Hebrews that encourages us to keep running the race, since we "have not yet resisted to the point of shedding your blood" (Heb. 12:4).

And if all of that is not strange enough, Christ-lovers live for another world and can't wait for Him to appear to take them there to be with Him forever. In fact, Christ affirms that there is a special reward, the "crown of righteousness" for all who *love* His appearing. (James 1:12). Note that it is a reward for righteous living, which, as we have learned, makes a lot of sense. Christ-lovers reside in the territory of His love; the territory of all that is right and good. When you look forward to your lover's return, you live in a state of being constantly ready for Him to show up (1 John 3:1–3). And so our love drives our hearts to long for that day. But not in a disabling way. We are called to do well here on earth and need enough earthside focus to be faithfully successful. After all, Christ does expect us to enjoy life and not pine away a lifetime as a star-crossed lover. Yet underneath all that, Christ-lovers live with one eye to the sky.

In my book *Eternity* I told the story of the children at the Shepherds Home in Union Grove, Wisconsin. My friend Bud Wood is the founder and developer of what has become one of the finest homes for mentally challenged children and adults in America. Many of the residents of Shepherds Home are afflicted with Down's syndrome and are minimally educable. The staff at Shepherds makes a concentrated effort to present the gospel to these children. As a result, many have come to believe in Christ as Savior and in a heaven that will be their home.

Bud told me that one of the major maintenance problems at Shepherds is dirty windows. I had expected him to say fingerprints on walls or mud in the hallways, but I was not ready for what he said next.

"You can walk through our corridors any time of the day," Bud explained, "and see some of these precious children standing with their hands, noses, and faces pressed to the windows, looking up to see if Christ might not be coming back right then to take them home and make them whole."

The simple, uncomplicated minds of these children have much to teach us. We should be asking ourselves, when was the last time we cast a glance toward the sky to see if this might not be that long-awaited moment when we finally will see Christ face-to-face?

To a self-consumed world whose existence is defined by the boundaries of birth and death, of cash and comfort, a Christ-lover's life will look a little off the screen of normality. But these things are not abnormal to us. Nor are they strange to the One we love. While loving Christ leads us to radical expressions of living and responding to life, unlike earthside love, the assumed risks never materialize. His love for us and our loving responses to Him are secured by the fact that He works everything together for good for those who love Him (Rom. 8:28). Because He loves us, He never wastes our sorrows. Knowing that, we are able to love Him freely and securely without reservation.

And this is just the point. Loving Christ motivates us to express our love to Him in concrete ways that defy other people's expectations. Traditions and even religiously contrived patterns of behavior don't stand in its way. When love is authentic, there is something wonderful and real about it that strikes a sense of curious interest among those who watch it unfold.

Unless we, like Simon, are among those who have forgotten that they too have needed to be forgiven much. Who in our goodness have grown to love ourselves and the systems that affirm our all-rightness more than we love Christ. Who are so bound in tradition that there is no room to rejoice in spontaneous fresh winds of love from an untutored heart. Who have not yet tasted the joy of life at Jesus' feet.

AFTER ALL HE'S DONE FOR ME

Adolf Hitler was obsessed with the eradication of the Jewish race. To be a Jew in Europe in the 1940s was a dangerous condition, because they were hunted relentlessly and sent to concentration camps and gas chambers. Their crime? They were, through no fault of their own, born Jewish. When the Germans took Denmark, Hitler demanded that all the Jewish Danes wear a yellow armband to mark them for the express purpose of deportation to a concentration camp. Legend has it that the king of Denmark, Christian X, was forced to read the decree from the balcony of the Amalienborg Palace. And then, with tears in his eyes, the king proceeded to put a yellow armband on his own arm for all to see.

Tradition has it that all the Danish people followed, making it impossible for the German forces to carry out their horrid intentions against the Jews of Denmark.

We. through no fault of our own, have been born sinners. With the mark of sin indelibly imprinted on our lives, our adversary hunts and intends to destroy us. And he would—except for the stunning reality that the King of Heaven came to live among us. With tears in His eyes, He placed the armband of our sin on Himself as He suffered a cruel and unjust punishment. And all this so that we might forever be safe from our enemy, eternally hidden in His matchless love.

The sinning woman is one of us. And we are one with her. Though suffering the disgrace and humiliation of Simon the Pharisee's judgment, she found an advocate in Jesus, her forgiving Savior. He willingly placed the armband of her sin on Himself that she, too, with the rest of us, might live forever free.

For this and for all the rest of the abudance of His grace on our loves, how can we help but gladly love Him forever!

Love so amazing, so divine,
demands my life, my soul, my all.

NOTES

Chapter 1—At Jesus' Feet

[1] James McBride, *The Color of Water: A Black Man's Tribute to His White Mother* (New York: Putnam/Riverhead Books, 1996), 42–43.

[2] Ibid., 165.

[3] Ibid., 50.

[4] Ibid., 217.

Chapter 2—Love the Way It Was Meant to Be

[1] Oscar Wilde, *De Profundis* (published posthumously in 1905; quoted in *Encyclopedia of the Self* by Mark Zimmerman), www.authorslibrary.org.

Chapter 4—Simonized Saints

[1] Enzo Noe Girardi, *The Complete Works of Michelangelo* (New York: Reynal and Co., 1966), 552, 554.

[2] Margie Haack, "Journey to the Stake," *World*, March 15, 1997.

[3] Adapted from the video *The Brooklyn Tabernacle Live: He's Been Faithful* (1994).

Chapter 5—The Pharisee in All of Us

[1] Oswald Chambers, *My Utmost for His Highest* (Grand Rapids: Discovery House, 1992), June 19.

[2] Roy Clements, Sting in the Tale (Leicester, U.K.: Inter-Varsity Press, 1995), 78–79.

[3] A. M. Hunter, *The Gospel According to St. Mark,* Torch Bible Commentary (London: SCM, 1967), 40–41.

Chapter 6—Barriers to Love

[1]*Milk and Honey* (newsletter), December 1997, and *Current Thoughts and Trends* (periodical), April 1998, 21.

[2]Barbara Ehrenreich, "What a Cute Universe You Have!" *Time,* August 25, 1997.

[3]Ibid.

[4]Jerome Miller, *The Way of Suffering: A Geography of Crisis* (Washington, D.C.: Georgetown University Press, 1988), 151.

Chapter 9—The Ultimate Testimony

[1]Philip Yancey, *What's So Amazing About Grace* (Grand Rapids: Zondervan, 1997), 11.

[2]Will Durant, *Caesar and Christ* (New York: Simon & Schuster, 1944), 602.

Chapter 10—Street Love

[1]John Grisham, *The Street Lawyer* (Garden City, N.Y.: Doubleday, 1998), 9–10.

[2]Used by permission of Craig Phillips.

[3]Leo Tolstoy, "Where Love Is, God Is" (written in 1885; edited in electronic form by Harry Plantinga in 1995), www.qconline.com/online/martin.html.

Chapter 11—Betrayal

[1]Peter L. Berger, *A Rumor of Angels: Modern Society and Rediscovery of the Spiritual* (Garden City, N.Y.: Doubleday Anchor Books, 1990), 24–25.

Chapter 12—After the Party

[1]C. S. Lewis, *The Problem of Pain* (New York: Touchstone Books, 1996).